#TEACHERS SERVETOO

#TEACHERS SERVETOO

The Unraveling of Educational Frontlines

EVAN ERDBERG

Founder of Proximity Learning Inc.

Published by RESULTS Faster! Publishing

2591 Lakeside Parkway, Suite #200, Flower Mound, TX 75022

ISBN: 978-1-956370-19-5

Printed in the United States of America

Disclaimer: The information provided in this book is for general informational purposes only. The authors and publisher are not engaged in rendering legal, accounting, or professional advice. Readers are encouraged to seek professional advice before making any business decisions.

Contents

Acknowledgments

My passion is education. I'm a TK . . . a teacher's kid. In fact, both my parents were/are teachers. As the founder of Proximity, I live and breathe the education world seven days a week. I'm very thankful this book is finally in print. Let me acknowledge that a team of people, contributors, reviewers, and more helped shape and build this tool. I want to thank them all and recognize that this work was a team effort.

Thank you, the reader, in advance for considering an investment of your time to read, ponder, and reflect on #TeachersServeToo. My team and I would appreciate you telling others about it and recommending it on social media. Join our movement to acknowledge, appreciate, and thank all teachers, even if you are one, for serving and impacting our youth.

Preface

Imagine a classroom where learning transcends the confines of traditional textbooks and where teachers have at their disposal tools that unlock the full potential of every student. This book will take you on a journey into such classrooms, where educators are not just instructors but visionaries, and technology is not just a tool but a catalyst for profound change.

In the ever-evolving world of education, I've had the privilege of being a part of a journey that's as diverse and dynamic as the students we serve. Over the span of more than three decades, I've been immersed in the exciting blend of passion, expertise, and innovation that fuels this field.

My story in education began with a fervent belief in the potential of technology to revolutionize learning. Armed with this belief, I embarked on a career that took me through a series of roles in public education. Along the way, I found my true calling and forged deep connections with school districts and educators who share my commitment to student success.

My mantra has always been simple yet powerful: every student is unique, and education should be tailored to meet individual needs. This belief has driven my work, pushing me to advocate for differentiated learning—a concept that's at the heart of what I do. I've specialized in developing and implementing software and services that adapt seamlessly to the diverse requirements of schools, regardless of their size.

In my thirty-year journey, I've worn many hats in education— working with reading and mathematics, offering tutoring services, and facilitating supplemental educational programs. But my true passion lies at the intersection of education and technology. It's an intersection that holds limitless promise, and I've dedicated my career to unlocking its potential to enrich the educational experiences of students. My journey has afforded me unique insights into the fusion of education and technology, and it's this wealth of experience that I bring to the pages of this book.

Now, as a contributor for this book, my role is to shine a light on the incredible stories of educators who have left an indelible mark on the world. These are the real authors of inspiration, and I'm here to underscore the pivotal role of educational technology in their journey.

The Background

The world of education is constantly evolving, shaped by the needs and aspirations of both students and educators. This book is a celebration of those who have embraced change, leveraged technology, and dedicated themselves to the betterment of education. It's a tribute to the unsung heroes of classrooms, schools, and districts who have harnessed the power of educational technology to transform the lives of countless young learners.

The Purpose

Teaching today isn't just about imparting knowledge; it's a relentless balancing act on a tightrope strung between education and survival. Imagine standing in front of a classroom, your back to a world where mass shootings lurk like shadows, where students—once eager learners—may now pose a threat or not even show up to class, where the weight of unrealistic expectations sits heavy on your shoulders.

Every day, teachers are forced into a dual role: educator and potential peace officer. They're tasked not only with igniting young minds but also with safeguarding their own lives and those of their students. It's an unthinkable burden to carry. They're expected to be both nurturing mentors and defenders against the unthinkable.

In an age where the sanctity of a classroom has been shattered by violence and by the ramifications of the worst event to ever negatively affect education—COVID. Where the once-revered figure of a teacher now faces the stark reality of being a target, the profession has become a high-stakes gamble with safety. It's a profession where educators are forced to contemplate strategies for surviving an attack while trying to foster a love for learning, even when the student population has embraced absenteeism.

This isn't just about arming teachers with textbooks; it's about arming them with the tools to navigate a landscape fraught with danger and disillusionment. The inherent risks of being a teacher today have turned what was once a noble pursuit into a hazardous occupation, leaving educators grappling with a chilling truth: in a world where they're meant to inspire hope, they're forced to face fear head-on.

Within these pages, you'll delve into the courageous narratives of modern educators who, amid the digital renaissance, navigate a landscape where innovation intertwines with unprecedented challenges. Their stories aren't just about embracing technology but are a testament to survival in an educational sphere where safety concerns loom large. As these educators harness the power of educational technology to craft groundbreaking learning experiences, they simultaneously confront the harsh reality of today's classrooms—a reality tainted by the looming threat of violence and the immense weight of unrealistic expectations.

Evan Erdberg: A Visionary in Education

Evan Erdberg is a name synonymous with innovation and excellence in the world of education. With over sixteen years of online K–12 and higher education sales and human capital management experience, Evan has left an indelible mark on the educational landscape.

As the president and founder of Proximity Learning Inc. (PLI), Evan has led the charge in revolutionizing K–12 education through virtual teacher staffing. PLI stands as an industry-leading company, acting as the human resources (HR) backup plan for over 100 school districts nationwide. Evan's vision and dedication have resulted in the placement of thousands of qualified teachers in vacant classrooms, ensuring that students across the country have access to quality education.

Prior to his role at PLI, Evan held a director-level position at Teachscape, where he managed one of the largest implementations in the country of principal certification and teacher evaluation systems that incorporated student data. His expertise in educational technology and teacher evaluation systems has contributed significantly to the improvement of education quality and teacher development.

Evan Erdberg's journey in education is characterized not only by his extensive experience but also by his unwavering commitment to enhancing educational outcomes. His visionary leadership and dedication to leveraging technology to improve learning experiences have earned him a well-deserved reputation as an incredible force for positive change in the field of education.

Evan's contributions to the educational sector continue to inspire and pave the way for a brighter future in education. His relentless pursuit of excellence, coupled with his profound understanding of the intersection of technology and education, make him a true trailblazer in the field. We are honored to have Evan Erdberg as a vital contributor to the world of education.

Acknowledging Influences

I am deeply grateful to the countless educators, administrators, and technologists I've had the privilege to work with over the years. Their dedication and commitment have shaped my understanding of education's potential, and I owe much of my inspiration to their tireless efforts.

Preface

As someone who has spent a lifetime advocating for teachers in America, this book reflects my passion and unwavering belief in the power of these heroes to transform education for 180,000 children annually.

A Glimpse of What's to Come

The book is structured to take you on a journey through the experiences and insights of these remarkable educators. Each chapter unveils a different facet of the educational landscape, showcasing the diversity of approaches and the transformative outcomes they have achieved.

The future of learning is about leveraging instructional innovations to create more engaging, effective, and equitable educational experiences. As we navigate this evolving educational landscape, technology will be a driving force, opening doors to new horizons and unlocking the full potential of learners worldwide. Embracing the possibilities that technology offers is not just a choice, it's an imperative for the future of education and the ability to ensure every student gets access to the teacher they deserve when one is not located in their school.

I invite you to join me on this enlightening journey. As you read these stories, reflect on these heroes who have dedicated their lives to shaping young minds and the boundless potential that lies ahead.

Thank you for embarking on this literary adventure with me. Together, we will celebrate the heroes of education and the dynamic tapestry they weave. Let's honor their dedication and explore the world of educational technology, where innovation meets inspiration, and learning knows no bounds.

Dr. Michael Robinson,
Vice President of School Partnerships

Introduction

My journey to starting the education technology company Proximity Learning Inc. began long before I envisioned ever running an edtech startup. I grew up immersed in teaching, with both parents dedicating their lives to the profession. My mother spent over twenty-five years as a middle-school special-education educator. Some of my earliest memories involve tagging along as she prepped classrooms, crafting imaginative bulletin boards, and arranging welcoming desks for her future students. She could never stop worrying and prepping for her students on weeknights, weekends, and even in the summer season. Her dedication to her students and to her family never ceased to amaze me.

My father was a businessman and entrepreneur and later served as a professor in the MBA program at Long Island University—in addition to building two companies. Late nights, never-ending stress, impending doom, imposter syndrome, self-doubt, addiction to caffeine, more late nights, followed by early mornings, so little sleep, and the desperation to find funding are just some of the words that come to mind when I think about the entrepreneurial experience. I saw much of this when I was a teenager at home while my father was starting his first business. Fifteen years later I better understand what my father was going through. I never fully grasped the risks my father had taken in leaving a stable job until I did it myself. I'm not sure if the trait is something that is passed down from parent to child, but I do want my children to understand what it is like to be an entrepreneur. The public just sees the success stories that all seem like overnight successes. The reality is, it takes years of hard work, dedication, and a little bit of luck to create a product that solves a real problem and that people are willing to invest money in.

Witnessing my parents' relentless commitment left a profound impression on me. I witnessed firsthand the long hours they invested after school and on weekends, doing lesson planning and grading assignments, to provide the best educational experiences possible for the students. I accompanied my mother on back-to-school shopping sprees where she enthusiastically stocked up on supplies for creative hands-on learning activities, rarely complaining about digging into her own paycheck. The teaching life became ingrained in me at a young age.

Given my upbringing, I assumed most classrooms across America mirrored the devotion I saw in my parents. So when I later stepped into my first professional role traveling to schools nationwide, the reality I encountered was jarring. Instead of vibrant communities of passionate teachers, I discovered half-empty teacher workrooms filled with despondent teachers and unstaffed classrooms.

After school hours ended, I asked the principals, "Where are all the teachers?" Their response was universal: "We haven't been able to find the teachers we need for years." This shocking teacher shortage predated the pandemic by at least a decade. Yet, it seemed to be an open secret in education, largely invisible to those outside the field. I refused to accept this status quo. In my mind, there had to be better solutions.

After speaking directly with administrators, teachers, counselors, parents, and support staffs across the country, the deep systemic issues plaguing our education system came into focus.

Exceptional teachers were leaving the classroom in droves, disillusioned and burned out. Students were paying the price, losing electives and enduring overcrowded classes taught by exhausted substitutes. While technology radically disrupted nearly every industry, education remained stubbornly antiquated.

I envisioned an edtech solution capable of connecting qualified teachers to students anywhere, while providing flexibility and personalization. Virtual classrooms could allow teachers to deliver individual attention and forge meaningful relationships regardless of geography. By leveraging technology, we could revolutionize education, make teaching sustainable, and engage all types of learners. Proximity Learning Inc. was born out of my desire to tackle the teacher shortage crisis, spark innovation, and bring equity to millions of students nationwide.

The Movement America Needs for Our Future: #TeachersServeToo

As I was traveling all across America, I couldn't shake this nagging feeling, this blatant imbalance in how we recognize service. It hit me square in the face: why do teachers get the short end of the recognition stick compared to other heroes like our military and medical pros? I mean, seriously, while these incredible folks enjoy year-round perks, educators are left out in the cold, only getting a shout-out during "back to school" madness or during a fleeting week of appreciation. It's like their service is an afterthought, or worse, invisible.

We're in the middle of a screaming shortage of teachers, yet their tireless efforts are brushed aside or acknowledged like a once-a-year novelty. That's just not right. So, I thought, why not shake things up? #TeachersServeToo isn't just a catchy phrase, but a full-blown movement—a wake-up call to society's selective amnesia. It's high time we gave these unsung heroes the props they deserve—not just once in a blue moon, but every single day.

This isn't about token gestures; it's about recognizing the heart, sweat, and soul teachers pour into shaping young minds. And believe me, facing a teacher shortage of epic proportions, it's crystal clear that we need to champion their cause.

My rallying cry isn't just about hashtags, it's a battle cry. It's time to turn the spotlight on these everyday superheroes and show some serious love for the game-changers who light up our future.

#TeachersServeToo aims to flip the script, rallying everyone to honor, cele- brate, and appreciate teachers' dedication, 24/7, 365 days a year. Join the movement, because it's time to give these educators the respect and recognition they rightfully deserve.

I've noticed on multiple occasions that the individuals in the teaching profession did not garner the same attention or respect as other service-led jobs. #TeachersServeToo became a way of simply recognizing the service of teachers, not only as government employees when working in the public-school sector, but also just within the profession in general.

After reading a sign at a retail store offering discounts to service members in the military and medical professions year-round, I wondered why educators weren't offered the same kinds of perks, benefits, or recognition for their daily sacrifices.

Educators were only recognized for their contributions maybe once or twice a year, during "back-to-school" time in the fall or during teacher appreciation week. How strange; why did their service only matter one or two times a year, if it was recognized at all?

At a time when the nation is seeing a massive teacher shortage, doesn't it matter now more than ever to recognize that their profession should be recognized as a job "in service" to others? #TeachersServeToo is about leading a movement that recognizes the profound service that the teaching profession entails and motivating others to observe the service of teachers year-round.

The following chapters will delve deep into the flaws plaguing our education system, as well as my vision for the future. But first, we must closely examine the factors pushing public schools to the breaking point and why reversing the mass teacher exodus is an urgent priority. The stakes could not be higher for our students and our nation's future.

Hostile Factors Public-School Teachers Are Facing Today

"At Least 19 Children, 2 Teachers Dead After Shooting at Texas School"—ABC News

Introduction

The fact that we're witnessing a surge in students attacking their own teachers is beyond alarming—it's downright gut-wrenching. What does it say about our education system when educators, who should be revered as mentors, are now becoming targets? It's a harsh slap in the face, a wake-up call to the grim reality lurking within our schools.

Bill Maher said it best: "If humanity can impose rules on warfare, let's do something really ambitious. Let's try them in high schools because our public schools are no longer safe for the teachers. A third of teachers in America say they've been harassed or threatened, and one in seven in this country has been physically attacked. They're bitten, they're beaten."

This isn't just a matter of isolated incidents; it's a symptom of a much deeper malaise festering within our society. We've created an environment where the authority of teachers is challenged and where respect for those shaping our future is fading into oblivion. And let's not kid ourselves, this isn't solely the fault of students. It's a collective failure, a system that's failing to protect its educators and, by extension, its students' right to a safe learning environment.

"Surviving a School Shooting: Impacts on Mental Health"—
Stanford Institute for Economic Policy Research

"This Is Not the Job We Signed up to Do"—*Education Week*

Let's just sit with these for a moment. These are not just headlines; they are stark reminders of the trauma etched into the very fabric of our education system. Imagine being a student or a teacher, or just imagine being a human being navigating a world where the threat of a school shooting isn't a distant nightmare but a chilling possibility. It's not just about physical survival; it's also about the mental scars that linger long after the chaos subsides.

And then we've got, "This Is Not the Job We Signed up to Do." Education Week didn't mince words there. It's like a collective cry from teachers across the nation, screaming out that something's gone terribly wrong. Educators aren't just facing the challenges of teaching; they're thrust into a battlefield where safety concerns, lack of support, and overwhelming expectations turn their noble profession into a daily struggle.

In a book diving into the controversial realm of teacher expectations and the #TeachersServeToo movement, the headline, "6-Year Old Shoots Teacher at Virginia Elementary School," hits hard. It's like a sudden jolt, thrusting us into the harsh reality teachers face every day.

A classroom, a place meant for learning and growth, is suddenly turned into a scene of unimaginable chaos. It's a chilling reminder of the heavy burden teachers carry—not just as educators, but as frontline guardians of safety in an increasingly unpredictable world.

As we navigate these controversial teacher expectations, this headline screams out for attention. It's a stark wake-up call, shouting about the unrealistic pressures placed on our educators. They're expected to be superheroes in the classroom as protectors against the unthinkable.

Doris Santoro, a professor of education at Bowdoin, wrote by e-mail in response to a New York Times query regarding the morale of public school teachers:

> *Teachers are not only burnt out and undercompensated, they are also demoralized. They are being asked to do things in the name of teaching that they believe are miseducational and harmful to students and the profession. What made this work good for them is no longer accessible. That is why we are hearing so many refrains of, "I'm not leaving the profession; my profession left me."*[1]

It's time for a reality check, America. These headlines aren't just stories; they're mirrors reflecting the deep-rooted issues we've swept under the rug for too long. If we continue down this path of neglect and indifference, we're not just jeopardizing the quality

---

1 https://www.nytimes.com/2022/12/14/opinion/teacher-shortage-education.html

of education, we're failing our students, our teachers, and the very essence of what education should be: a safe haven for learning and growth.

This tragedy echoes the very essence of #TeachersServeToo. It's a flashing red signal demanding that we acknowledge and support teachers not just once or twice a year but every single day. These headlines aren't just a news flash, they are a rallying cry for change. It's time to reevaluate these expectations and provide the necessary resources and recognition for those tirelessly serving our communities within the education system.

We are starting the movement #TeachersServeToo to finally give teachers the respect they deserve. You will see this hashtag throughout this book and when you do, we encourage you to take a moment and recognize a teacher on social media, in an e-mail, or even by a hand-written note. Let's change society's discourse about teacher service and remind this world that teachers are on the frontlines to impart knowledge to America's children.

When you meet a military service member,
you typically thank them for their service.
As well we all should.
But when you meet a teacher,
the typical response is, "I'm so sorry."

Section One

Education as We Know It

As progress dawns, education stands at a crossroads between tradition and transformation. Our understanding of education has grown beyond the classroom, embracing lifelong learning across age, culture, and borders.

Over time, the schoolhouse became a knowledge center where eager minds gathered under mentors. The twenty-first century brought technology and a new schooling paradigm. From dusty textbooks to the digital interface, information flowed continuously and was accessible at a fingertip.

It has not all been sunshine and rainbows; debates have evolved with the Internet age. Screentime's effects on young minds, the digital divide's exclusion, and the loss of interpersonal skills in the quest of pixels have all raised concerns. A delicate balance is needed to acknowledge benefits while protecting learners' entire development.

As we enter the future, education's story is unwritten. The canvas awaits creativity and insight. Once limited to four walls, the classroom now spans the world. The once solo teacher now inspires collaboration. The student, once a vessel to fill, is now an unknown adventurer.

Chapter One

The Importance
of Learning

If you are planning for a year, sow rice;
if you are planning for a decade, plant trees;
if you are planning for a lifetime, educate people.

Chinese Proverb

With public school enrollment on the decline, some education experts are beginning to question whether investing in school staffing is even the best choice. Funding public education has always been an illusory task with very little transparency, despite the fact that much of this funding is directly contributed by taxpayers. The saga continues as the post-pandemic era has heightened or created even more spiraling in the education sector.

When it comes to understanding the teacher-shortage crisis, it sounds counterintuitive to plan for expected future teacher layoffs and dwindling public school enrollment numbers, but it's already begun. There are many indications of this, including chronic absenteeism, safety, the mismanagement of funds, backwards formulas that are decades old that determine how funds are allocated to public school districts, and my personal favorite, use-it or lose-it rules. This means that once the school year formally ends on June

30th, schools don't get to keep any money they have left over. Their budget actually gets reduced by the amount they did not spend the following year. This prompts increased spending at the end of the school year on products that have nothing to do with helping our children learn and wastes billions of taxpayer dollars annually.

The Crucial Role of Free Public Education

Education is a cornerstone of societal progress, shaping the minds of individuals and driving the advancement of communities and nations. The provision of free public education emerges as a vital element that not only ensures equal opportunities for all but also fosters economic growth, social mobility, and the cultivation of an informed citizenry. Free public education is one of the most important things we can provide as a society to our citizens.

However, it is clear that not all schools are created equal in the land of opportunity. It might sound completely counterintuitive, but public schools and public education are being set up to fail so that the corporatization of education can be implemented in an effort to show that access to education for all was somehow a mistake and not a fiscally sound institution.

> Not all schools are created equal in the land of opportunity.

The Importance of Learning

We cannot let this happen. We can't allow public education to become a market-driven space where only the best and most profitable schools survive. While there are most definitely struggles and systemic issues to solve, we can't let access to free public education disappear. Instead, we need to create the programs and tools necessary to make sure every student has equitable access and every student is successful.[2]

The importance of learning and teachers' roles in this process cannot be overstated. For most US children, it is in public schools that they will not only learn reading and writing skills, mathematics, and other core content, but this might be the only place they can access learning for additional durable skills that will be with them throughout their lives.[3]

Durable skills, often referred to as "soft or transferable skills," are the versatile and enduring abilities that transcend specific job roles and industries. These skills provide the foundation for success in various contexts by enhancing a person's adaptability and effectiveness. Communication skills, for instance, enable individuals to convey ideas clearly, fostering collaboration and understanding on the job. Critical thinking and problem solving empower individuals to approach challenges with creativity and logic, leading to the creation of innovative solutions.

Therefore, teachers are not merely teaching students content in the public school system, they are also teaching them skills for life and addressing their social and emotional needs throughout the acquisition of these durable skills.

I've been fortunate enough that my first group of students that I taught are now full-grown adults. I've had the good fortune of interacting with them, and I've heard firsthand the impact

2 https://www.mwera.org/MWER/volumes/v29/issue4/V29n4-Hall-COMMENTARY.pdf

3 https://americasucceeds.org/defining-durable-skills

I had on them and their lives. They often tell me, "You held me accountable, but you also saw me as a person, a complex individual." And so, now I really try to strike a balance between school and life for my students.

Dr. Anna Stubblefield, superintendent of
Kansas City Public Schools

Equal Access and Opportunity

Free public education levels the playing field, or at least it should. An equitable, free public education should be ensuring that every child, regardless of their socio-economic background, has access to quality education. By eliminating financial barriers, it prevents educational inequality from taking root and perpetuating the cycle of poverty. A society that provides free education demonstrates its commitment to social justice, empowering individuals to rise above their circumstances and pursue their dreams. Teachers are expected to shoulder social justice issues and advocacy while maintaining strict guidelines to academic standards and closing learning gaps.

In Little Rock, we have this model called community schools. As is the case in most urban cities across our country, a little over 70 percent of our students are impacted by poverty. So, when you think about Maslow's hierarchy of needs, our core business is teaching and learning, at the top of the pyramid. However, kids are coming to school without the bottom levels satisfied: coming to school hungry, without clothes to wear, issues with having food security in their homes, worrying about their light bill or where they're going to stay or even medical care.

To address this, we've implemented a concept called community schools where we really want our schools to be the hub of the community. So this is where everybody comes to get help, services, and support for anything that they need. We have eight community schools now with health, medical, [and] dental clinics within the schools. We have thriving pantries where communities and folks from the neighborhood come to get food items once a week. We have all types of mental health and counseling services available, not just for students, but their families. And in some cases, due to the type of partnership we have with the providing agencies who's providing medical or dental services, those services are available to the entire family. And so, we are removing all types of barriers that a lot of families have that prevent their children from being able to really focus and take advantage of what public schooling is supposed to offer.

This aspect of service that they're being provided has really made a difference in their lives and has made it easier for the children to be able to focus on the thing that is most important, and that's their education. And so hopefully, over time, those students will be equipped to where they could break those generational cycles of poverty, [so] that when they leave us, that they'll be prepared and equipped and ready to have a different lived experience.

Dr. Jermall Wright, superintendent, Little
Rock School District

Economic Growth and Innovation

Education is a cornerstone of economic development. A skilled and educated workforce is more productive and innovative, contributing to economic growth and competitiveness on a global scale. By offering free public education, society invests in its future human capital, equipping individuals with the knowledge and skills needed to drive technological advancements and solve complex challenges. Oddly enough, there are direct correlations with economic issues and the roles of teachers. In the public eye, teachers are vilified or treated antagonistically when demanding more for their students and speaking candidly about the inequities of the system and the way it's funded. During the pandemic, teachers were expected to go back to teaching in person despite the risks, because it was necessary to "get things back to normal" for economic mobility and growth.

Social Mobility

Free public education should serve as a ladder of upward mobility, enabling individuals to transcend their upbringing and achieve higher socioeconomic statuses. Without the burden of tuition fees, talented students from disadvantaged backgrounds can pursue higher education and secure better job prospects, breaking the cycle of intergenerational poverty. This phenomenon not only benefits individuals and families, it also uplifts entire communities. Whether or not they are given the credit for this, teachers are agents for social mobility and social change simply because they teach.

Informed and Engaged Citizenship

A well-functioning democracy relies on an informed and engaged citizenry. Free public education fosters critical thinking, civic awareness, and an understanding of societal issues. Citizens who are knowledgeable about their rights and responsibilities are better equipped to participate in democratic processes, make informed decisions, and hold their leaders accountable. This, in turn, strengthens the fabric of the nation and supports good governance. Teachers take on the additional responsibility of supporting the idea of free thought and independent forward thinking.

Social Cohesion and Diversity

Public education provides an environment where children from diverse backgrounds come together, fostering social cohesion and cultural understanding. By interacting with peers from different walks of life, students learn to appreciate differences, develop empathy, and build bridges across societal divides. Teachers support this learning experience and contribute to a more harmonious and integrated society.

Long-Term Benefits for Society

Investing in free public education yields long-term benefits for society as a whole. Educated and literate individuals are more likely to lead healthier lives, engage in civic activities, and contribute positively to their communities. Also, an educated workforce attracts investment, encourages entrepreneurship, and stimulates innovation, thus driving economic prosperity and development. Teachers are helping to build a better society through education, as well as passing down knowledge that will have far-reaching effects for decades to come.

Access and Equity Are Key

Free public education stands as a cornerstone of societal progress, enabling equal access, promoting economic growth, nurturing social mobility, and fostering an informed citizenry. By investing in education, societies invest in their own future. It is a commitment that reaps rewards in the form of social cohesion, economic development, and the empowerment of individuals to reach their full potential. As we continue to navigate the complexities of an ever-changing world, the importance of providing free public education remains steadfast, ensuring that opportunities for growth and advancement are within reach of all, regardless of their background or circumstances.

Teaching has been institutionalized. Each year, the focus turns to more standardized tests and data-driven results, while funding is wasted in millions to billions of dollars each year. What a shame. The love of learning cannot be institutionally driven. It takes teachers with heart to create life-long learners. I'm not saying we have to kibosh the whole system, but it's madness to keep doing the same thing and thinking it will achieve new results. We have to stop this downward spiral and regroup. It's time to break free of the institution and evolve our classrooms.

The importance of providing free public education remains steadfast, ensuring that opportunities for growth and advancement are within reach of all, regardless of their background or circumstances.

The Rise of Public Education

The seventeenth and eighteenth centuries witnessed the emergence of public education systems, particularly in Europe. As nations sought to create well-informed and loyal citizens, state-controlled educational institutions were eventually established. This period also saw the spread of compulsory education laws, making attendance mandatory for certain age groups.

The Industrial Revolution brought significant social and economic changes. With the rise of industrialization, there was a growing need for an educated workforce with basic literacy and numeracy skills. Mass education systems were then created to meet this demand, and the concepts of age-based grade leveling and standardized curricula were introduced.

The twentieth century saw the expansion and diversification of educational institutions. The establishment of kindergarten, primary schools, secondary schools, and universities became more prevalent. Governments took on larger roles and oversights in funding and monitoring education, emphasizing the importance of education for national progress and economic growth.

Amid the chaos of our times, teachers stand tall, shouldering the weight of education on their shoulders. They're not just instructors; they're mentors, counselors, and heroes navigating uncharted waters. But where's the spotlight on these everyday superheroes? Throughout the pandemic, they've pivoted tirelessly, mastering remote teaching, while battling their own fears. Yet, society overlooks their sacrifices, and the lack of support leaves them feeling stranded. We're on the brink of losing these beacons of knowledge if we don't start recognizing their worth. #TeachersServeToo

Modern Challenges and Critiques

While institutionalized education has undoubtedly made education more accessible to the masses, it has also faced several criticisms. Some critics argue that the focus on standardized testing and rote memorization stifles creativity and critical thinking and falls short in preparing students for postsecondary options. Others criticize the system's tendency to perpetuate social in equalities and neglect individual learning styles.

Institutional education broadened access for all, but over time new legislation and legal ramifications have fenced in creativity and critical thinking. Our teachers deserve to be treated as professionals and the one-size-fits-all approach often leaves students unprepared for their paths ahead while overlooking individual learning styles, perpetuating inequalities. In America

> *we have the most diverse neighborhoods in the world, where schools support 100 different languages while homeless students sit next to celebrities. Our students deserve a school system to meet their needs no matter their background.*
>
> Micah Ali, president of
> Compton Unified School District

Technology and Online Education

With the advent of the Internet and digital technologies, education has experienced a new revolution. Online learning platforms and Massive Open Online Courses (MOOCs) have provided unprecedented access to education worldwide, challenging the traditional brick-and-mortar institutions and opening new avenues for learning.

Education has evolved from informal apprenticeships to highly structured and standardized systems in the form of institutionalized education. While it has significantly contributed to societal progress and individual development, ongoing efforts are necessary to address the challenges and ensure that education remains relevant, inclusive, and equitable in the rapidly changing world.

Think being a teacher is a walk in the park? Think again. These incredible humans juggle more than just lesson plans. They're dealing with ever-changing curricula, diverse classrooms, and now, health concerns in the pandemic. The pressure is real, folks. And the worst part is that their efforts often go unnoticed. The lack of respect and resources is pushing these superheroes to the edge. We're risking losing the backbone of education—passionate, dedicated teachers who give their all every single day. #TeachersServeToo

Chapter Two

Post-COVID-19 Learning

The evidence is now in, and it is startling. The school closures that took 50 million children out of classrooms at the start of the pandemic may prove to be the most damaging disruption in the history of American education. It also set student progress in math and reading back by two decades and widened the achievement gap that separates poor and wealthy children.[4]

In the aftermath of the COVID-19 pandemic, the landscape of education has undergone profound transformations, sparking discussions across diverse population perspectives. As we navigate this uncharted territory, one resounding message echoes throughout: teachers, the unsung heroes of the education system, deserve utmost respect and appreciation. They have demonstrated unwavering dedication, adaptability, and resilience, enriching the lives of their students despite the unprecedented challenges. This introductory exploration will delve into the multifaceted world of post-COVID learning, shedding light on the various perspectives that shape it, while shining a spotlight on the educators who remain steadfast in their commitment to nurturing the minds of future generations.

---

4   *The New York Times,* The Startling Evidence on Learning Loss Is In, Nov. 18, 2023.

Alright, let's dive into how this global curveball—COVID-19—has shaken up the education scene. It's like a plot twist that no one saw coming, leaving everyone from teachers to parents, publishers, and students in a whirlwind of change.

Teachers: The Unsung Heroes

Teachers? They've been on the frontlines of this rollercoaster. Overnight, they had to master the art of virtual instruction, turning their living rooms into classrooms and their laptops into teaching aids. Thirty-seven percent of teachers and 61 percent of principals reported being harassed because of their school's policies on COVID-19 safety measures, or for teaching about race, racism, or bias during the first half of the 2021–2022 school year.[5] As if that weren't enough, it's been a mix of late-night lesson plans, virtual office hours, and finding new ways to connect with students through screens. The impact? They've emerged as true heroes, adapting their teaching styles and navigating uncharted waters like champs.

> *Teachers aren't just in classrooms; they're on the frontlines of shaping futures. They battle ignorance, nurture curiosity, and mold minds all while often going unsung for their daily heroics.*
>
> Dr. J. R. Green, superintendent of
> Fairfield County Schools

Parents: The Unexpected Partners

Now, let's talk about parents. They suddenly found themselves wearing multiple hats as part-time teachers, tech support, and playtime buddies. It's been a juggling act, trying to balance work and home while ensuring their kids keep up with their studies. And let's be real, it hasn't been a walk in the park. But it's also forged a unique

5　https://www.rand.org/pubs/research_reports/RRA1108-5.html

partnership between schools and parents, giving rise to a new level of involvement in their child's education journey.

Parents need to own their actions, stop blaming teachers, and accept the universal truth that they and their child are the ones responsible for their learning. "There is no teacher, no matter how skilled, who can teach a student who does not want to learn" (William Glasser). Too many children start school without even the most basic social skills that includes how to even go to the bathroom, respect for adults, and not to bite your peer. Parents are responsible for raising their children and how they act outside the house, teaching them right from wrong, respect for others, respect for authority, self-worth, and discipline.

Teachers can't teach if the students do not respect them. Teachers can't teach if they can't build trust. Teachers can't teach if they are always on the defensive and can't have a partnership with each parent to where they can have an honest discussion.
Parents need to take ownership. They can't just send their children to school and expect the teacher to teach them decorum and how to read.

Sorry parents, this might hurt to hear, but your child is NOT perfect. With three young children of my own, I understand this. They are perfect angels and can do no wrong in my wife's and my eyes—but are they? There must be a true partnership between parents and teachers for quality education to succeed. Show me a strong PTA and I will show you a successful school!

Publishers: Pivoting Perspectives

Publishers? They had to switch gears too. Traditional textbooks? Well, they took a back seat. Digital resources became the star of the show, with publishers racing to provide engaging online content that kept up with this new reality. It's like they hit fast-forward on innovation, bringing interactive learning experiences right to students' screens.

> There must be a true partnership between parents and teachers for quality education to succeed. Show me a strong PTA and I will show you a successful school!

Students: Navigating New Horizons

Last but not least are the students—the true heart of education. They went from bustling hallways to virtual classrooms, mastering the art of online collaboration and independent learning. It's been a journey of adaptability, resilience, and finding their voice in this digital realm. They've discovered that learning doesn't stop even when the world hits pause.

It's been a wild ride, with educators, parents, publishers, and students each stepping up in their own unique way. It's shown us that education isn't confined to four walls; it's a dynamic force that can adapt, evolve, and thrive—even in the face of a global shakeup.

> # Education isn't confined to four walls; it's a dynamic force that can adapt, evolve, and thrive—even in the face of a global shakeup.

Embracing the Future of Education:
Navigating the Virtual Instruction Landscape

In the realm of education, the tides of change have surged with the advent of virtual instruction. The days of monotonous "click click next" screens and asynchronous learning are numbered in an educational landscape that's grappling to retain both teachers and students. It's crystal clear that expecting students to merely log in, switch on their cameras, and feel enthusiastic about learning won't cut it if personal connections to teachers and content are missing. That's where the real potential lies for improvement, even as we navigate the virtual realm. Even if classes find their home online, they can and should be engaging and downright fun. The keys to unlocking this are found in live teachers, dynamic lessons, and a curriculum grounded in standards. This trifecta holds the potential to create substantial ripples in the world of education, and the time has come to bid farewell to the old ways of doing things and embrace a future that's ripe for innovation.

> The keys to unlocking engaging and fun classes are found in live teachers, dynamic lessons, and a curriculum grounded in standards.

Amid the relentless waves of the pandemic, virtual instruction has emerged as a formidable contender in the post pandemic era. It demands a pragmatic assessment of the value it brings to students, educators, and school districts alike. Yet, as the pandemic unfolded, we witnessed many grappling to adjust to this new paradigm, raising pertinent questions about its viability.

For school districts aiming to harness funds through initiatives like the Elementary and Secondary School Emergency Relief Fund (ESSER), the strategic inclusion of a robust, virtual element is nothing short of crucial. However, it's imperative to understand that merely transplanting traditional curricula onto a Zoom call won't yield effective results. Drawing from my perspective as a digital education entrepreneur, it's evident that this is where many districts encountered the greatest challenge during the pandemic. The attempt to retrofit a curriculum designed for asynchronous learning into a comprehensive virtual instruction model led to suboptimal outcomes, underscoring the need for a dynamic online curriculum that's purpose-built for virtual instruction.

As local educational authorities contemplate the road ahead, they're met with fundamental questions that shape the future of education. What does education look like in the next few decades? How do we devise a strategic blueprint that aligns with instructional practices and long-term district objectives? While each school district may take distinct routes in seeking answers, I firmly believe that there are three universal steps to be taken to prepare for the future and provide top-tier virtual education.

1. **Embrace the Inevitable: Virtual Education Is Here to Stay.** Let's get one thing straight—virtual education isn't just a fleeting experiment; it's a formidable game-changer. The decrease in available teachers across the nation, coupled with limited financial resources, might drive school districts toward embracing virtual education as a central pillar of future instruction. While the initial investment might seem daunting, the long-term benefits are substantial. But it all begins with an essential step— acknowledgment. All stakeholders, from teachers, to parents, to administrators need to embrace virtual education as a steadfast reality, not a temporary fix.

2. **Invest in Skillsets for a New Era.** The future of education demands a fresh perspective on teacher training. The era of textbook-centered and asynchronous learning is fading, making way for a new breed of educators armed with specialized skills. Blending online resources seamlessly with direct instruction is the cornerstone of student success, and teachers need to be equipped accordingly. Establishing technology-driven professional learning communities can serve as a robust foundation for educators to adapt and thrive in this evolving landscape.

   As technology evolves and generational attitudes toward virtual domains shift, seismic changes in instructional formats are imminent. In the next two decades, substantial shifts in academic and financial resource allocation are virtually inevitable. Teachers are no longer confined by geographical limitations; the challenge now is to establish virtual academic best practices.

Investing in digital training and its integration should be a cornerstone of teacher professional development.

3. **Forge a Curriculum Primed for the Digital Realm.** Crafting a curriculum fit for the digital age is no small feat—it requires a comprehensive overhaul. Physical textbooks and simple online uploads won't suffice. The blueprint for a dynamic online curriculum goes beyond superficial adaptations. It involves meticulous planning, reimagining content delivery, and creating engaging experiences. Enter tools like Quizlet for gamification, Nearpod for interactive content, and virtual reality labs that bring lessons to life. The key lies in crafting a curriculum that leverages technology to deliver a world-class learning experience.

The National Virtual Teacher Association (NVTA) emerges as a valuable resource, offering training to teachers seeking fluency in virtual instruction. Their free and paid programs empower educators to navigate this evolving landscape. Establishing a robust online curriculum isn't a short-term endeavor, it's a multi-year journey aimed at fostering dynamic, engaging, and effective online learning experiences.

In the grand theater of education, the spotlight is now on virtual instruction. As the curtain rises on the future, educators, administrators, and stakeholders must join forces to shape an educational landscape that's equal parts innovative and impactful. It's a journey marked by acceptance, skill-building, and curriculum evolution, a journey that heralds a promising era of education reimagined.

Imagine educators meeting their students through the captivating lens of holographic technology. It might sound like a page ripped from a science fiction novel, but as we forge ahead, educational leaders are tasked with gripping the reins of our collective instructional future. The path forward demands a steadfast commitment to charting our course, recognizing structural deficits, and shoring up institutional vulnerabilities to pave the way for students in an ever-expanding global economy.

Decline in Enrollment: A Harbinger of Change

The 2020 pandemic's aftermath has unveiled a sobering reality—approximately 1.2 million students have departed the public school system, as per a recent national survey. While this 3 percent plunge isn't the steepest decline in US history (that distinction belongs to 1943 during WWII), a teacher shortage now looms on the horizon.

While some families turned to homeschooling or private schools that braved the pandemic storm, there remains a cohort of students whose enrollment, both in-person and online, remains unaccounted for. This raises a pertinent question: What's become of these students, and are they receiving any education at all?

It's about time we give teachers the respect they deserve. They're not just educators; they're the architects of our future. The pandemic threw a spotlight on their resilience and revealed a system that doesn't appreciate their dedication. We need to step up, folks. It's more than a pat on the back, it's about proper support, resources, and acknowledging their pivotal role in shaping society. Without this, we're risking losing the very people who inspire and nurture future generations. #TeachersServeToo

Educators and community leaders brace yourselves; these numbers should set off alarm bells. The fiscal implications of dwindling enrollment numbers are a looming concern for school districts, especially those serving the most vulnerable and marginalized communities. Beyond financial woes, the data speaks volumes about a growing lack of confidence in the public school system itself.

We live in a country that does not adequately prepare black children, Latinx children and poor children. I think there are people who benefit from a class of children, namely children of color being uneducated, particularly in a capitalistic society where you've got to have owners and servers. If you are not intentional, the workers will always come from the poor and from people of color and the owners will be predominantly white,

> *predominantly affluent class. And so recognizing that, I think that we have to train people to figure out how to navigate the politics and secure the power to advantage children and people that have been historically denied access and opportunity. So while less than 6 percent of the population of superintendents in this country are black or Latinx, Howard's mission is to help change that trajectory.*
>
> Dr. Shawn Joseph, Assistant Professor/
> Co-Director of Urban Superintendent
> Academy, Howard University

Recovery Starts Within: A Beacon of Hope

It's high time we shift our gaze inward for solutions. The treatment of teachers before and during the pandemic warrants a serious appraisal. We needn't scour outside classrooms for fixes, the path to progress lies within. Teachers and school districts require unwavering support now more than ever. The aftermath of the pandemic has ushered in a new reality—classrooms are filled with students who are grappling not only with academic hurdles but also social and emotional challenges. The urgent need for remediation and support echoes across the nation, with many students returning with educational gaps of up to two years. As leaders, our responsibility is clear: we must rally behind recovery efforts on all fronts, with a keen focus on initiatives that uplift and empower teachers. Here's a glimpse into some strategies, informed by years of entrepreneurial experience in education.

1. **Cultivate a Culture of Positivity and Optimism.** An often-overlooked cornerstone—nurturing a welcoming and optimistic environment—costs nothing but reaps profound rewards. People naturally gravitate toward places where they feel valued and part of a community. It's time for leadership to initiate a mental shift and translate values into tangible actions within the workplace.

2. **Streamlining for Success: Reducing Redundancy.** Let's free our teachers from the burden of needless redundancies. Initiating candid "ditch" meetings where departments trim superfluous initiatives can lighten the load. In the face of a mass exodus from education, teachers cannot be expected to shoulder additional responsibilities. It's incumbent upon leadership to shoulder this burden.

3. **A Community Effort: Outreach to Recover Students.** The task of recovering missing students shouldn't rest solely on teachers' shoulders. A coordinated endeavor involving administrators, social workers, counselors, and the community at large is essential. Establishing a task force dedicated to reclaiming these students, ensuring their return to the classroom or virtual space, is a critical step.

4. **Equitable Funding: Nurturing a Supportive Ecosystem.** Sustaining public education demands proper funding that recognizes and rewards talent at every juncture. Adequate funding for educational technology is equally pivotal. The sink-or-swim narrative must give way to a culture of support. Innovative, out-of-the-box thinking can revolutionize the public school sector, empowering teachers, students, and families.

5. **Embracing Innovation: Crafting a Dynamic Curriculum.** The shortcomings of rushed virtual learning during the pandemic are glaring. The education tech sector has learned its lessons, offering a bridge between the teacher shortage and dwindling student enrollment. Armed with training, updated technology, and tailored online curricula, the journey toward a new era of education is set in motion. By partnering with education tech companies and harnessing their tools, we can usher in a new dawn of online learning that caters to the evolving needs of students and educators alike.

Our collective journey is marked by a relentless pursuit of progress, be it through embracing technology, reimagining curriculum, or nurturing a supportive ecosystem. The path forward is illuminated by a shared commitment to nurturing the educational landscape, one that prepares students for an interconnected world and empowers educators to guide them along this exhilarating journey.

COVID Response and Education Outcomes

The COVID-19 pandemic presented numerous challenges worldwide; it was a public health issue that impacted economies, democratic institutions, health care, and education. Many countries, including the United States, were unprepared for the long-term challenges of providing education for students and the lasting effects of COVID for the foreseeable future. The education of American students post-COVID-19 reflects a need to recalibrate public school education. Students have fallen behind, and years later they are still struggling to catch up and fill the learning losses they experienced during the pandemic.

Districts used ESSER funds to finance staffing during the pandemic. But they didn't plan for it to go away. Now, districts are faced with tough fiscal decisions. When their funding is up, they won't be able to maintain their faculty and staff. They should have focused on innovative programs to challenge the shortage to lessen their dependence on an expensive "in-house" staffing solution. Instead, many just gave raises that tax dollars could not sustain. Teachers are still leaving the classroom, and now there are even more worries on the horizon.

As the founder of a virtual-learning platform, I saw firsthand that many public-school institutions attempted to implement ad hoc virtual instruction programs utilizing a variety of Internet-based platforms. Many of these programs were implemented quickly out of necessity and thus were prone to numerous failures. These failures included lapses in security, broadband or low bandwidth, and difficulties implementing programs whereby students were fully engaged in the day-to-day instruction. These inadequacies were largely a manifestation of failing, long-term strategic plans created by public schools and a gross lack of training and understanding of the learning management systems or educational platforms. The twenty-first-century classroom commands a variety of instructional and curricular-blended learning and conventional pedagogy that is often ignored by traditional public-school districts.

The impact of the pandemic on education, particularly virtual learning, has indeed been profound and complex. One of the foremost challenges was the difficulty in building meaningful relationships and the heightened awareness of existing inequities, especially in communities of color.

The shift to virtual learning brought to the forefront several critical issues:

- *Relationship Building: Virtual environments made it challenging to foster the same level of personal connection that physical classrooms allow. Teachers and students struggled to create strong, supportive relationships, which are essential for effective learning and emotional well-being.*

- *Preparedness of School Leaders: Many school and district leaders found themselves navigating uncharted waters. The sudden shift to virtual learning required quick adaptation, often without adequate resources or training, leading to increased pressure and stress.*

- *Technological Divide: The pandemic highlighted the digital divide in stark terms. Students in districts with 1:1 device programs, where each student receives a device for learning, could adapt more quickly compared to those in districts without such resources. This divide often disproportionately affected communities of color, exacerbating existing educational inequities.*

- *Inequities in Education: The pandemic didn't create educational inequities, but it certainly magnified them.*

> *Students from underserved communities faced more significant challenges, from lack of reliable internet access to inadequate learning spaces at home.*
>
> *As we move forward, it's crucial to reflect on these challenges and work towards more equitable and effective educational solutions. Leveraging the lessons learned during COVID-19 can help in creating a more resilient and inclusive educational system. We must re-imagine education so that we are better equipped to address these issues in a post-pandemic world.*
>
> Dr. Victoria Hansen Stockton, superintendent
> of Bellwood School District 88

As we move forward, local educational authorities must reevaluate their instructional priorities to adapt to future health emergencies and modern challenges. Irrespective of these specialized problems, there is a critical component of the American classroom that must be revisited. Should we keep setting the expectation of a ratio that is not the most effective model for student learning? For the most part, schools are typically designed around the thirty-to-one teacher ratio, but is this really an effective model for teaching emergent generations of students? From my perspective, this student-to-teacher equation is unlikely to be effective as the sole approach to the future student or America as a whole.

Additionally, the nature of teaching and learning must evolve in correlation with advancing technologies. The United States and other international educational entities must be compelled by the very nature of the success of virtual instruction. There must be a push to develop and adopt standards, alignments, and rubrics that lay out the best practices of the virtual classroom and how students can more successfully engage with teachers in this instructional modality.

As our country emerges from the COVID-19 pandemic, we need to be open to engaging with the future of instruction, which I believe could include a blend of traditional classroom learning and virtual programs. Twenty-first-century students require adaptable and individualized approaches. And teachers need the time, virtual training, content skills, and support to help create the best lessons and deliver content effectively across virtual platforms. Therefore, leveraging technology and accessibility to experienced teachers is a requirement — not a request—in the modern American classroom.

Instruction in this blended-learning approach must reflect the needs of all students, including those who require alternative instructional methods. Facilitating blended learning for those students who work well on their own, or are socially risk-aversive and need the opportunity to explore curriculum on their own, reflects the individualized instruction that all students and parents crave. Delivering instruction through an adaptive model can elicit results that reflect a broader spread of student demographics and achievement. Instructional pedagogy can only be enhanced by the lessons learned for a more meaningful and thoughtful elegant design to student learning in the twenty-first-century.

Blended approaches can provide classroom equity and instructional choice and access across the nation. Furthermore, devoting more resources, especially on a national level, to foster an enhanced program design that continuously monitors and improves the development of virtual instruction resources is essential to confronting teacher shortages, lack of student access, and parental involvement. In the long-term, as a nation, we must be prepared to confront not only *if* another emergency occurs, but *when*.

Opportunity abounds with an open mind to virtual instruction and the myriad of learning choices for students. By adopting the virtual classroom as a valid and reliable means of delivering instruction, we are more able to efficiently design student programming and deliver a standard of instruction that not only meets but exceeds learning expectations for students. Efficiency and affordability in terms of teaching and learning can become a natural by-product by blending virtual and traditional pedagogy.

As a nation, we were vastly underprepared for the challenges of COVID-19. This global health crisis revealed the foundational cracks in our instructional paradigm and created scenarios that made the workloads of teachers completely unmanageable and unfair.

We cannot ignore the lessons learned over the past few years.

We need to reallocate resources and use our human adaptability to prepare not only for a health or environmental emergency but also for a relevant and necessary reexamination of our instructional models in order to promote the educational health of our civilization. Every single student deserves an equitable education. And teachers deserve our respect and support.

By designing a meaningfully robust and multipronged educational system that treats virtual teaching as valid and reliable, we ensure our long-term social, academic, and cultural survival.

Brace yourselves, there's a storm brewing in education. Teachers, the unsung heroes, are contemplating walking away for good. It's not just about paychecks, it's about respect and a nurturing work environment. The pandemic brought safety concerns to the forefront, and teachers are feeling the strain. We're staring at a cliff's edge here, folks. If we don't start making some serious changes—acknowledging our teachers' worth and fixing a broken system—we're setting ourselves up for an educational disaster. #TeachersServeToo

Section Two

Differentiation: One Size Doesn't Fit All

Just like no two snowflakes are the same, no two students' minds are exactly the same. This is a very important truth in education, where the one-size-fits-all method is slowly giving way to the idea that people have different ways of learning and different needs.

The traditional picture of a classroom with rows of desks and a single teacher at the front may have been useful for many generations, but it can no longer cover the wide range of skills and interests that people have. A single plan can't capture the essence of a young artist who thrives through visual expression, a young scientist who finds comfort in experimenting, or an eloquent speaker who grows through discussion and conversation.

As pedagogy grows, teachers are becoming more and more open to the idea of diversity. Once a single tune, the art of teaching has become a symphony of changes that fit the different beats of each student's mind. Teachers and organizations are changing the way education works because they see that there are many ways to learn. Personalized learning plans, flexible curricula, and interdisciplinary methods are the new building blocks for making room for the different ways people learn.

In this ever-changing world, teachers become growth facilitators who enjoy the task of changing their methods to help the seeds of brilliance that grow in their classrooms. Once a student knows something, the teacher becomes a guide who shows the way, while letting the student explore, find, and build.

Chapter Three

Educational Equity

If a child can't learn the way we teach,
maybe we should teach the way they learn.

Michael J. Fox

H ave you ever seen someone wear so many hats at once? That's a
teacher for you. They're not just educators, they're counselors,
motivators, and sometimes even superheroes without capes. But
here's the kicker: while they're busy shaping young minds, they're
also navigating through a minefield of challenges. The pandemic?
They aced the transition to online teaching like pros, risking their
health to keep the education flame burning. But where's the recognition? Where's the support? It's high time we started valuing
these warriors properly before they decide to hang up their capes for
good. #TeachersServeToo

In the digital age, educational equity has emerged as a critical
issue in ensuring that all students have equal access to quality education and opportunities for success. While technology has opened
new avenues for learning and engagement, it has also highlighted
the stark disparities that exist between students with varying levels
of resources and support. In this landscape, teachers play a pivotal

role in bridging the digital divide and promoting educational equity. Their expertise, dedication, and empathetic approach are indispensable in tailoring education to meet the diverse needs of students, fostering a nurturing learning environment, and empowering young minds to thrive in an ever-evolving world. As we navigate the challenges and opportunities presented by the digital era, recognizing and valuing the crucial role of teachers remains paramount in creating an equitable and inclusive educational landscape for all.

Reform initiatives such as teacher evaluation improvements, curriculum enhancements, and increases in teacher accountability over the last 30 years in the United States have not done much to improve public schools overall, nor have they created meaningful outcomes in terms of student achievement. So what can public schools do to meet the standards of the newest generation of students? Let's refer to them as "iGen." In my observations, the current nature of teaching and learning in public schools is predicated on what students many generations ago required to be successful. The way many schools conduct teaching and learning is directly linked to a nineteenth century model of instruction. That would suggest that the demands of students haven't changed since the 1890s.

How can we create problem solvers if we take that approach?

> Schools today lack the innovation necessary to cater to the specific and differentiated needs of students in modern society.

The concept of equity has taken center stage in the modern educational landscape. Reports highlighting significant economic disparities underscore the considerable barriers that students face in terms of access and opportunities within schools. Public schools serve as vital environments where students refine their cognitive, social, and competitive proficiencies, preparing them for their forthcoming careers and the challenges of the workplace. It's evident that students who are deprived of adequate resources might inadvertently miss out on a comprehensive twenty-first-century education.

> *Something that I really try to hold fast to regardless of what role that I'm in, is understanding that the reason we're here is to provide an equitable education to students. And so students have to be at the forefront of everything that we do. And it's again, easier said than done in a field where you need adults to do the work to get kids where they need to be. There's a balancing act that must be played to make sure that the needs of kids are actually being served and the needs of adults are being served, but not to the detriment of the needs of students.*
>
> Dr. Jermall Wright, superintendent Little Rock School District

Taking this perspective into account, let's explore a set of practical measures that leaders within the education industry could contemplate.

Fostering Innovation. In the landscape of any organization, enacting reforms can prove to be challenging, particularly when the goal involves introducing logical enhancements that challenge the established norms. Placing emphasis on fostering innovation, leveraging technology, and nurturing organizational development has the potential to yield substantive solutions to the issues highlighted earlier.

Professional Learning Communities. As stewards of the educational realm, it's imperative that we reconsider the methodologies employed for teacher evaluation, as this factor can play a pivotal role in driving the transformation of public schools. Over the past decade and a half, attempts at reforming teacher evaluation have unfolded with varying degrees of success. The most promising models seem to hinge upon the establishment of professional learning communities (PLCs) that facilitate the mentorship of new educators, while simultaneously upholding and demanding a high standard of instructional excellence from all teachers, irrespective of their experience.

Educator Buy-In. For leaders championing reform-oriented pedagogical approaches, the endeavor should encompass the formation of a cohort of like-minded educators who rally behind an innovative reform agenda. When executed authentically, democratic frameworks of participation create an environment in which teachers sense their meaningful contribution to positive outcomes. Cultivating buy-in from educators stands as a pivotal determinant of success.

Differentiated Virtual Instruction. When it comes to shaking things up in education, public schools can tap into the power of fancy tech and strong internet connections. Imagine using video chat platforms to bring in teachers from far and wide. That could really jazz up the learning journey for students, don't you think? And hey, let's not forget about giving each student their own special learning plan. Like, tailoring the lessons to fit what they're awesome at and where they could use some polishing. That kind of personal touch could seriously set them up for big-time success down the road. But here's the cool part: by jotting down a unique plan for every student, it's not just the kids and their parents who win—the whole gang in the community, including the folks who chip in through taxes to support schools, can keep tabs on how everyone's doing. Teachers, principals, and schools would all be on the hook for celebrating victories, tackling setbacks, and making sure those awesome accomplishments keep piling up.

Listen up, folks, because these suggestions are no joke. Our public schools are on the hot seat, and everyone's watching. If we don't tackle the issues in our schools, we're basically rolling the dice with our futures and our students' futures too. We're talking serious stuff here, the ups and downs of the economy and how it affects the "haves" and the "have nots." But don't sweat it, because with some smart planning that's all about improving and being creative, we can totally soften the blow and make sure our students get what they need.

Imagine being able to deliver high-quality educational access to students in rural and urban communities online who did not have it before — a feat we actually accomplished in spite of the pandemic. Now imagine if we could expand that reality and provide high-quality content, instructors, and learning management systems regardless of students' socioeconomic backgrounds, achievement levels, or locations. How would this change education? Furthermore, how would this change our communities and society at large?

All children have the right to an equitable education. As leaders in the ed-tech industry, if we are part of a society that turns a blind eye to disadvantaged and vulnerable student populations by allowing unfair, unjust, low-funded, and inequitable schools to fail these students, then we are communicating to these groups that they do not matter.

> *It's very dangerous now to lead in a way that tries to change the trajectory of historically minoritized and historically marginalized children. I believe there are powers that benefit from the status quo that don't want education fixed for certain races and classes of children because if you fix the situation, then you won't be investing in the remediation services that some of these entities provide. I believe that there are people who benefit from crises and want a crisis so they can sell their solutions. And in that context, fixing a problem goes against their economic proposition of making profits off of the failure of black and brown children. It is essential that the superintendent works with the board to establish the moral imperative and to establish what they're going to do first, second, and third, because any superintendent that moves faster than his or her culture will fail.*
>
> Dr. Shawn Joseph, Assistant Professor/
> Co-Director of Urban Superintendent
> Academy, Howard University

In this modern age, we have the tools, the technology, the knowledge, and the means to provide kids with innovative and exciting educational opportunities through virtual learning. It's time to be disruptive to the archaic educational institutions and ask ourselves and each other, "What can we do better now? Furthermore, how can we do this without devouring the public school sector and instead offer supportive solutions to the teacher shortage and ever-growing dropout rates in rural and urban school districts?"

Funding and Fairness

According to Education Northwest, "Data on district funding across the country has confirmed that high-poverty schools receive less money than more affluent schools within the same district and across districts."[6] As leaders in the industry, we need to make sure funds are adequately being used to fund high-quality academics, no matter where schools and student populations are located.

Access to ed-tech can't be something only suburban communities receive. We have a responsibility to serve students in rural and urban communities and ensure they have the same access to the same high-quality curriculums seen in other communities. If we see certain communities are consistently facing challenges or gaps in service, we need to reach out to administrators, parents/families, and school district boards and show them how we can fill those gaps.

We have to make sure districts, teachers, and parents/families see the value in what we provide as the education tech industry grows. It's up to us in the ed-tech industry to be as transparent as possible and communicate what technology can do for their students, teachers, and communities as a whole. Time and time again, the research shows students do the best learning with teachers they can connect and build rapport with. It's this human connection ed-tech leaders seek to support and help thrive.

In the past, schools focused on the "equality" initiatives, not realizing they were completely missing the equity piece in the way their schools were run. While it is clearly important to acknowledge our shortcomings and past mistakes, the next and most important step toward building a more equitable future for the education industry is to have radical visions and goals for what that looks like.

6   "The People in the Numbers: Rethinking Data for Black Student Success." *Education Northwest*, 1 Mar. 2021, educationnorthwest.org/insights/people-numbers-rethinking-data-black-student-success.

> *We need to avoid looking at children's education from a deficit standpoint where we work to attempt to fix the children. Instead, we need to focus on understanding the assets that each child brings and working to build upon the assets and the strengths that children naturally possess.*
>
> Dr. Shawn Joseph, Assistant Professor/
> Co-Director of Urban Superintendent
> Academy, Howard University

We must push ourselves and each other to build something better and more sustainable. We must push ourselves to build better systems and technology to bring to these centers of learning. And we must push ourselves and build communities to make this vision accessible for all, especially the most vulnerable rural and urban communities of students.

We have everything we need to make these visions a reality, but we have to put words into action. Our task is not easy and yes, it will take time, but we have to lead the way in order for others to see by our examples and become just as passionate about putting students first.

Chapter Four

Five Common Education Myths

If you have always done it that way, it is probably wrong.

Charles Kettering

If you asked a hiring manager at a given company about remote work options the year before COVID, most would say it was not an option. Now, you would be hard pressed to find a company that does not offer some type of remote work. Similarly, most university professors teach through Zoom, with assistant professors left in the classrooms to grade tests and assign work. COVID normed the world to virtual instruction and virtual work. For the first time, the whole world saw the power of Zoom, Microsoft teams, Google meets, and many other video delivery platforms. In addition, the population grew to expect remote options. The problem we all face is one around quality and how to create opportunities online that mirror person-to-person contacts.

Years later, in the ever-evolving world of education, the chatter around virtual learning has ignited quite the debate. You have folks questioning its effectiveness and others worried about missing out on social interaction. And then, there are the ongoing myths: Is virtual learning just a passing fad? Will tech glitches rain on the learning parade? But through all this, there's a solid truth that stands tall—a heartfelt salute to the educators who've not just adapted but also stuck by their students through thick and thin.

So, let's dive into these myths and unravel them one by one. As we do, we'll also shine a light on these dedicated educators, celebrating their unwavering passion and expertise that continue to be the guiding stars for young minds, even in these times of transformation.

Shattering the Myths: Embracing the Reality

1. **Virtual Learning: Easier but Less Effective?** Okay, let's chat about this common notion that virtual learning is a walk in the park—simple and, well, kind of meh. But hold on a second, because that's not the whole picture. Virtual learning isn't just about clicking through slides and calling it a day, it's a vibrant world of possibilities that packs a punch. Learning isn't about the setting, it's about the substance. Whether you're in a traditional classroom or a virtual one, the heart of the matter is engagement and impact. It's not about just showing up, it's about showing up with a toolkit full of captivating strategies.

    So, you have your virtual-learning space. Now, imagine it as a playground where educators get creative. It's all about interactive quizzes, videos that take you on learning adventures, and discussions that spark fiery debates. Virtual learning isn't about taking it easy, it's about taking it up a notch.

So, when you think "virtual learning," don't just think "simple." Think "transformational."

Sure, it might not be the traditional classroom you're used to, but don't let that fool you. Virtual learning can be just as rigorous and just as impactful, maybe even more so.

It's all about shaking things up, embracing the digital frontier, and realizing that learning knows no bounds, whether it's in a classroom or on a screen.

2. **Isolation vs. Interaction.** Alright, let's tackle the elephant in the room—social interaction in virtual learning. Now you might think it's all isolation and lone-wolf vibes, but hang tight, because there's more to it than meets the eye. Sure, we're not in the same physical classroom, but that doesn't mean we're sitting in our own little silos. Imagine this: you have a bunch of students, each with his or her own digital space. And guess what? These spaces aren't just for jotting down notes, they're vibrant hubs of collaboration. We're talking about collaborative projects that make your brain cells do a happy dance. Think breakout sessions where students brainstorm, share ideas, and work together to crack problems wide open. And let's not forget interactive discussions that light up the virtual room with insights and debates.

So while we might not be face-to-face, we're definitely not alone in this digital world. It's like having a virtual playground where students meet, greet, and team up to tackle challenges. Those concerns about isolation? Well, they're like old news now. Virtual learning isn't a solo gig, it's a dynamic dance of minds coming together and forging connections that prove social interaction is alive and kicking even in this digital realm.

3. **Beyond a Trend/Sustaining Impact.** The pandemic kicked virtual learning into high gear, showing us that it can adapt and evolve, proving its worth for the long haul. Virtual learning is like a dynamic player that's stepped up its game thanks to the current circumstances. The pandemic threw us a curveball, and virtual learning caught it and ran with it. It's like the superhero

of education—rising to the occasion and showing its true potential. And guess what? This isn't just a one-hit-wonder. Virtual learning isn't here to make a quick appearance and then vanish into thin air. It's got staying power. So, when you think of virtual learning, don't just picture it as a fleeting trend. Think of it as an adaptable companion that's here to stay, ready to reshape and revolutionize education for the long run. It's not just a moment in time, it's a game-changer that's shaping the future of learning.

4. **Overcoming Tech Hurdles.** We've all been there, worried about those pesky technical hiccups that can pop up during virtual learning. But with some smart planning and strategic moves, we can actually keep these disruptions at bay. Think of it like plotting a course for a seamless educational journey. It's all about gearing up with the right tools and strategies to tackle any bumps that might come along the way.

   But here's where the magic happens—strategic implementation. It's like conducting a symphony where every instrument plays its part. From hardware to software, everything needs to be in sync. When tech is set up like a well-coordinated orchestra, it transforms from a potential roadblock to a smooth-sailing vessel that propels learning forward. The result? Technology steps up from being a stumbling block to becoming a valuable ally. It's like having your trusty copilot guiding you through the educational adventure. And here's the best part: when tech works seamlessly, it fades into the background, letting educators and students take center stage.

   In this ever-evolving world of virtual learning, it's not about dodging challenges, it's about tackling them head-on and letting technology be a dynamic force that propels us toward a future of enriched learning experiences.

5. **A Virtual Program Is Just Click-Click (asynchronous) Learning.** If you're aiming for a high-quality virtual-learning experience, don't just settle for asynchronous learning alone.

Research and experience show that asynchronous learning on its own can be a bit like learning in a vacuum. Sure, you're absorbing the info, but there's something missing. That missing piece? The live, real-time engagement that brings concepts to life, lets you ask questions, and sparks discussions. Synchronous learning is all about real-time, interactive sessions—live classes, discussions, and group activities. It's like being in a classroom, but virtually. And trust me, this is where the quality virtual program shines.

So the COVID-19 pandemic didn't just shake things up—it practically turned the education system on its head. The rush to virtual instruction? Yeah, that revealed a few chinks in the armor. Suddenly, planning and training gaps were front and center, leaving us all scratching our heads about fairness in access and quality. It's a clear reminder that the mission to offer top-notch education to every student calls for some serious adaptability. Because, let's face it, the unexpected can hit us anytime, and education should keep marching forward no matter what.

> *One thing that we as educators don't do well, is we don't adapt. Our education system is still based on this agrarian calendar and the ways in which we did things a hundred years ago. Sometimes we're very, very slow to adapt to changes, but technology is happening and moving at such a fast pace. We've got to learn how to adapt, take advantage of some of these advanced technologies that are out there, and find ways to where it can help our kids reach their potential and their goals.*
>
> Dr. Jermall Wright, superintendent
> Little Rock School District

As we envision the future of education, it is evident that a blend of virtual and traditional approaches is on the horizon. This necessitates a refined implementation of virtual programs grounded in a few critical elements:

Quality Technology: The Backbone of Virtual Learning. When it comes to virtual education, the quality of the technology is the secret sauce. We're talking about tech that's not just fancy, but user-friendly too. Think about it: smooth engagement and hassle-free interactions are what make the virtual-learning experience rock-solid.

Adaptable Educators: The Stars of the Virtual Show. Now onto the rockstars, our educators. Flexibility is their middle name, and they're nailing it. In this virtual world, they're the ones who've got the game-changing moves. They've taken their classroom expertise and are dishing it out in style, keeping things smooth and engaging for students. Whether it's a virtual classroom or a traditional one, these educators are setting the bar high.

> *Teachers invest not only in knowledge but in the well-being and future success of each individual in their care. Their service goes beyond the curriculum, shaping minds and hearts, nurturing a generation poised to make a difference.*
>
> Dr. Ingrid Grant,
> Chief of School Leadership
> for Henrico County Public Schools

Step into a teacher's shoes, and you'll discover a world of chaos, passion, and overwhelming responsibilities. From crafting engaging lessons, to managing classroom dynamics, and dealing with health concerns in a pandemic it's a rollercoaster. But here's the bitter truth: teachers' efforts often fade into the background noise of society. The lack of respect and resources? That's the final straw. We're looking at losing the backbone of our education system if we don't wake up and start showing these heroes some much-needed appreciation. #TeachersServeToo

Powering up with Professional Growth: The Key to Navigating Virtual Terrain. Let's not forget the magic potion behind it all: professional development. This isn't just your regular training—it's focused and tailored to empower educators in this ever-evolving landscape. We're talking about diving deep into the world of technology integration and crafting virtual classroom designs that hit all the right notes. With this kind of support, educators are striding confidently into uncharted territory, ready to steer their students toward a bright educational future.

Teachers deserve a standing ovation, a round of applause that doesn't fade away. They're not just imparting knowledge, they're shaping the leaders, thinkers, and innovators of tomorrow. But guess what? Society's not giving them their due credit. The pandemic highlighted their adaptability and dedication, but it also laid bare the cracks in a system that doesn't appreciate their sacrifices. It's time for a revolution, a shift in how we value and support these champions of education. Otherwise, we're waving goodbye to a profession that's the backbone of our society. #TeachersServeToo

A Testament to Resilience: Educator Stories

Amid these challenges, stories of success emerge. Educators have showcased remarkable resilience. Their commitment to forging connections, leveraging relationships, and delivering education with passion stands as a beacon of hope in these trying times. Virtual platforms, when harnessed effectively, create opportunities for students to access education they otherwise might not receive.

But hold on tight because we're heading toward an educational crisis. Teachers, these incredible souls, are contemplating an exit strategy. It's not just about better pay; it's about being respected and feeling safe at work. The pandemic added fuel to the fire, raising safety concerns and mental health issues. We're standing on the edge, folks. If we don't step up and show teachers that they matter, we'll be witnessing an educational catastrophe. #TeachersServeToo

A Glimpse into the Future:
Preparedness and Possibilities

We're still figuring out the full story of what the pandemic left in its wake. We're not just looking back, we're digging deeply into the lessons it's handed us. It made it crystal clear that we need some solid game plans in place for any additional curveballs headed our way.

Teachers are the silent architects of the future. They don't just teach, they mold minds, foster dreams, and inspire greatness. But here's the catch: while they're sculpting the leaders of tomorrow, they're also battling their own demons. The pandemic turned their world upside down, forcing them to adapt, innovate, and sometimes sacrifice their own well-being to ensure learning continued. Yet, the applause they truly deserve is drowned out by the deafening silence of a society that fails to recognize their monumental efforts. #TeachersServeToo

Picture this: a beefed-up education system with tech at its core, coupled with some top-notch strategies. That's the recipe for keeping the learning train on track no matter what storms roll in.

In this ever-shifting landscape, virtual learning isn't just a fleeting fad, it's like a superhero tool in an educator's toolkit. With dedication, innovation, and the ability to roll with the punches, educators are leading the charge toward a future where education is for everyone, come what may.

Chapter Five

Different Learning Styles

Wisdom is not a product of schooling
but of the lifelong attempt to acquire it.

Albert Einstein

Tell me and I forget, teach me and
I may remember, involve me and I learn.

Benjamin Franklin

Take a peek behind the scenes, and you'll witness a whirlwind of dedication, resilience, and sheer determination in every teacher's life. They're not just delivering lessons; they're managing diverse classrooms, dealing with administrative chaos, and now, navigating a pandemic minefield. The real kicker? Their efforts are often taken for granted. The lack of acknowledgment and support is pushing these superheroes to the brink. We're teetering on the edge of losing invaluable assets to education if we don't open our eyes and give them the respect they deserve. #TeachersServeToo

Differentiated learning styles, also known as learning modalities or learning preferences, refer to the idea that individuals have unique ways of processing and retaining information. These learning styles are thought to influence how a student best learns and understands new concepts and information. Understanding these learning styles helps educators tailor their teaching methods to cater to diverse students and individualized needs.

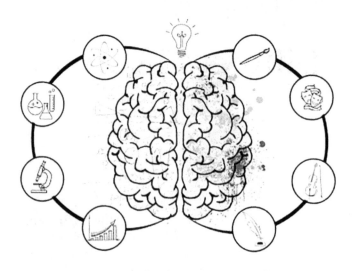

The popular model "VARK," which categorizes learners into the four main learning styles—Visual, Auditory, Reading/Writing, and Kinesthetic—was developed by Neil D. Fleming and Colleen E. Mills in the late 1980s.

The VARK model suggests that individuals may have a dominant learning style, a combination of learning styles, or a preference for different learning styles in different situations or subjects. All of this kind of information can help a virtual teacher and virtual learner target what works best for them in the online classroom.

Here's a brief overview of each learning style in the VARK model:

Visual Learners. Visual learners prefer to process information through images, graphs, charts, and other visual aids. They often benefit from seeing information presented in a visual format. Visual learners tend to remember what they have seen rather than what they have heard.

Auditory Learners. Auditory learners learn best through hearing and listening. They prefer spoken instructions and benefit from discussions, lectures, and verbal explanations. They may remember information by repeating it aloud.

Reading/Writing Learners. Reading/writing learners prefer to learn through reading and writing activities. They excel at processing written information and may enjoy taking detailed notes and writing essays or summaries.

Kinesthetic Learners (Tactile Learners). Kinesthetic learners learn best through physical experiences and hands-on activities. They prefer to engage with the material actively and learn by doing.

It's important to emphasize or acknowledge that many individuals exhibit a mixture of learning styles. These preferences can change depending on the subject matter or the context of learning. Instead of relying solely on one particular learning style, educators often use a combination of teaching methods to accommodate various learning preferences within a diverse classroom. Flexibility and differentiation in teaching approaches can create more inclusive and effective learning environments for all students, whether these are in the brick-and-mortar classroom or the online learning classroom.

Virtual Teachers and Learning Modalities

Virtual teachers, especially those trained and certified in virtual programming, have the tools and experience needed to effectively address different learning styles by employing a variety of teaching strategies and digital tools. Since virtual classrooms lack the physical presence and interactions of traditional classrooms, teachers need to be creative in their approach to cater to diverse learning preferences.

Here are some ways virtual teachers can address different learning styles:

Use Multimedia and Visual Aids. For visual learners, virtual teachers can utilize multimedia elements like slideshows, videos, infographics, and interactive presentations to convey information. These visual aids help engage visual learners and enhance their understanding of the subject matter.

Synchronous Learning Techniques

Build community
+ relationships

Lead interactive
modeling sessions

Small group
instruction

Personalized
teaching

Guided practice
+ applications

Create real time
conversations

Facilitate
collaboration

Ongoing +
timely feedback

Provide Verbal Explanations and Audio Resources. Auditory learners benefit from hearing information. Virtual teachers can record lectures, discussions, or audio explanations and share them with students. Additionally, they can conduct live online classes where students can listen to and participate in discussions and debates.

Incorporate Interactive and Hands-On Activities. For kinesthetic learners, virtual teachers can design interactive activities that involve students' active participation. These may include virtual labs, simulations, group projects, or hands-on experiments that students can perform at home using basic materials.

Offer Readings and Writing Opportunities. To cater to reading/writing learners, virtual teachers can provide reading materials, articles, e-books, and digital textbooks. They can also encourage students to write essays, summaries, reflections, or participate in online discussions and forums.

Provide Flexibility and Choice. Virtual teachers can offer students some autonomy in how they engage with the learning material. Giving students options to choose from various learning activities, projects, or assignments allows them to align their learning experiences with their preferred learning styles.

Utilize Gamification. Gamification can be an effective way to engage learners with different styles. Virtual teachers can incorporate educational games, quizzes, and interactive activities that allow students to learn through play.

Foster Collaborative Learning. Creating opportunities for group discussions, online debates, or virtual study groups can benefit different learning styles. This approach promotes social interaction and peer learning, appealing to various students' preferences.

Personalize Feedback and Support. Understanding each student's learning style can help virtual teachers provide personalized feedback and support. Individualized attention can enhance the learning experience and motivate students to stay engaged.

Encourage Reflection and Self-Assessment. Virtual teachers can encourage students to reflect on their learning preferences and strengths. Students can assess which methods work best for them and actively seek resources that align with their learning styles.

Continuous Assessment and Adaptation. Virtual teachers should regularly assess their students' progress and adapt their teaching methods accordingly. Analyzing students' performance and feedback can help identify areas where adjustments are needed to better accommodate different learning styles.

By incorporating these strategies into their virtual teaching practices, educators can create a more inclusive and engaging learning environment, addressing the diverse learning styles of their students effectively.

Besides addressing different learning styles (as discussed earlier with the VARK model), differentiated instruction refers to the practice of tailoring teaching methods, content, and assessments to meet the individual needs, interests, and learning styles of students. It recognizes that learners have diverse strengths and challenges, and a one-size-fits-all approach may not be the most effective.

Additionally, by incorporating the following forms of differentiated instruction into their teaching practices, educators can create inclusive and supportive learning environments that address the diverse needs of their students effectively:

Flexible Grouping. Teachers can create flexible groups based on students' readiness levels, interests, or learning profiles. This allows students to work with peers who are at a similar level or have similar interests. Grouping can be temporary, and students may switch groups based on their progress or changing needs.

Tiered Assignments. Tiered assignments provide different levels of complexity or depth for students to explore a topic based on their readiness and ability. Students can choose an assignment that aligns with their current level of understanding, allowing them to challenge themselves appropriately.

Learning Contracts. A learning contract is an agreement between the teacher and the student that outlines specific learning goals, activities, and timelines. Students have some autonomy in choosing the tasks they will complete to achieve the objectives. This approach promotes self-directed learning and personalizes the learning experience.

Choice Boards. Choice boards offer a menu of learning activities from which students can choose based on their preferences and interests. The activities may cater to different learning styles or multiple intelligences, allowing students to engage with the material in a way that suits them best.

Interest-Based Projects. Teachers can allow students to pursue projects based on their interests or passions. By incorporating students' hobbies or real-life topics into the curriculum, teachers can increase engagement and motivation.

Varied Learning Materials. Providing learning materials in various formats—such as written text, audio recordings, videos, and interactive simulations—accommodates different learning preferences and ensures that all students can access the content effectively.

Scaffolded Instruction. Scaffolding involves breaking down complex tasks into smaller, more manageable steps, and providing support to help students build their understanding gradually. As students demonstrate increased proficiency, the level of support can be gradually reduced.

Differentiated Assessments. Assessment methods can be adjusted to suit individual needs and learning styles. This could involve offering students options for how they demonstrate their knowledge, such as through presentations, written essays, creative projects, or oral examinations.

Technology Integration. Technology can enhance differentiated instruction by offering adaptive learning platforms, interactive simulations, and personalized learning paths. Educational apps and software can cater to individual learning needs and provide immediate feedback.

Varied Pacing. Allowing students to work at their own pace can be beneficial, especially in self-paced or online learning environments. Some students may need more time to grasp a concept, while others may progress more quickly.

Virtual teachers harness a diverse range of learning modalities to craft dynamic and engaging lessons that cater to various learning styles and preferences. By seamlessly integrating visual, auditory, and kinesthetic approaches, they create a well-rounded learning experience that resonates with students on different levels. Implementing best practices for engaging teaching, virtual educators leverage interactive tools, multimedia resources, and collaborative platforms to foster active participation and meaningful connections within the synchronous classroom. As technology continues to shape the educational landscape, these adaptable strategies enable virtual teachers to foster a rich and interactive learning environment that empowers students to thrive in the digital age. The twenty-first-century student craves connection and to be "seen." And this can only be achieved through real time live teaching.

No matter how far online technology or artificial intelligence has come, there is no substitute for an excellent live teacher.

Teaching is a science, it is not easy, and it requires patience, empathy, and the ability to truly build a unique learning plan for up to 180,000 kids a year. Until we as a population respect this job and, more importantly, the people who have devoted their lives to meeting our children where they are, we are going to continue to see the teacher shortage grow. The pandemic amplified the need for customized learning plans. While necessary, the extra work left many teachers emotionally and mentally drained. If we don't act fast and show them they matter, we'll be left with a void in education that will be felt for generations to come. #TeachersServeToo

Chapter Six

Inclusivity and Accessibility

Inclusion is not a matter of political correctness.
It is the key to growth.

Jesse Jackson

In the rapidly-evolving landscape of education, the principles of inclusivity and accessibility have become paramount for creating a truly equitable learning environment. As technology enables education to transcend geographical barriers and cater to a diverse range of learners, it also highlights the importance of addressing the unique needs and challenges faced by students with varying abilities and backgrounds. In this digital realm, teachers emerge as the cornerstone of inclusivity and accessibility as they possess the expertise and empathy to design inclusive virtual classrooms that cater to every student's individual learning styles and ensure that no one is left behind. By embracing innovative teaching approaches and leveraging technology thoughtfully, educators can bridge the gaps, promote diversity, and foster an environment where all students can thrive academically and personally.

As Executive Director Arizona School Board Association, I firmly believe in the imperative of meeting diverse student needs.

Schools, teachers, districts, and school boards must collectively commit to meeting students where they're at and supporting our teachers who are on the front line! It's not just an ethos; it's an obligation. Only by understanding and addressing the unique backgrounds, challenges, and aspirations of each student can we do what is right. Our educational ecosystem must be agile, responsive, and inclusive, ensuring that every student, irrespective of their journey, finds support, guidance, and opportunity. The only way to do this is to ensure we have the teachers there to guide these students. In an everchanging world we need to recognize teachers need to be placed on a pedestal, need to be respected, and need to be celebrated.

Devin Del Palacio, Executive Director, Arizona School Board Association and Former Arizona State Representative

How does diversity & inclusion impact the education sector?

Lack of diversity and inclusion is one of the main forces driving the Great Resignation. Employees are willing to hit the pavement in order to escape toxic work environments where they don't feel seen, heard or represented.

According to MIT Sloan Management review's survey based on 34 million online employee profiles, a toxic corporate culture is by far the best predictor of employee attrition.[7] The same source found three key factors that contribute to toxic company culture:

- Failure to promote diversity, equity, and inclusion
- Workers feeling disrespected
- Unethical behavior

7 Sull, Donald, et al. "Toxic Culture Is Driving the Great Resignation." *MIT Sloan Management Review*, 11 Jan. 2022, sloanreview.mit.edu/article/toxic-culture-is-driving-the-great-resignation.

Great Place to Work surveyed over 330,000 US employees, and those who said they didn't intend to stay at their current companies cited the absence of diversity, equity, inclusion, and belonging as key factors.[8] Employees considering leaving their current roles had repeatedly raised concerns about gender equity, fair promotions, fair pay, and equal versus limited opportunities. And significantly, employees who were members of underrepresented minority groups were most likely to leave.

So what are employees looking for in a work environment and job? What will make them stay? Unsurprisingly, diversity and inclusion are important here as well, particularly in their absence. While it's common to hear teachers rave about the immense purpose of their work, their love of showing up to teach, and the pride they have in their students, we need to make sure teachers can also talk about feeling represented, respected, and included in major decisions regarding the workplace.

Many educators will note they teach diversity and inclusion in the classroom every day, with strategic lesson planning and carefully selected texts for their diverse student populations. However, they aren't always seeing the same initiatives in school leadership or administration settings. For example, the Texas Association of School Boards (TASB) reports a gender gap in school district leadership: "Nearly three-quarters of all K–12 educators are women, but they account for less than one in five superintendents in Texas."[9] The report goes on to list the obstacles faced by women seeking superintendent jobs, including gender bias, subconscious preferences, self-removal, and family considerations, as potential reasons for this massive disparity.

---

8   Hastwell, Claire. "How Toxic Company Culture Is Driving Employee Turnover." *Great Place to Work*, 21 Apr. 2023, www.greatplacetowork.com/resources/blog/toxic-company-culture.

9   "This Is Why There Are Fewer Female Superintendents." *Texas Association of School Boards*, tasb.org/members/enhance-district/why-there-are-fewer-female-superintendents.aspx.

Sadly, the numbers for people of color in administrative or principal roles are often just as low and slow to climb as well. The National Center for Education Statistics released a report in 2018 comparing the distribution of public-school principals by sex and race/ethnicity between the school years 1999 to 2000 and 2017 to 2018 to see if there had been significant change in the numbers. While female representation had climbed 10 percent to account for approximately 54 percent of principal roles, representation of races other than white across the board were all less than 15 percent.

Sometimes people see the K–12 system not as a place whose primary mission is to educate children, but as a job factory. The school system provides hundreds or thousands of jobs. Sometimes, the people in charge see the money that comes into the system as a tool to provide contracts to their friends instead of the person that can do the job best.

Dr. Shawn Joseph, Assistant Professor/
Co-Director of Urban Superintendent
Academy, Howard University

This is unacceptable and is not what's best for students or teachers.

How can we do better?

First of all, this is a systemic and societal issue and, given the current times, clearly a "hot-button" topic. But regardless of controversy, we must continue to have difficult conversations around issues of race, gender, ethnicity, diversity, and inclusion, both in the historical record and in contemporary society. We must acknowledge that these numbers do not lie. There is great disparity and huge opportunities for growth. We need to take a hard look at our own biases and stigmas, and we all have them. Then, we need to make changes.

A great first step forward is to acknowledge the issue and then come up with authentic solutions that can help us provide nontoxic, diverse, and inclusive work environments for all people. We don't have to reinvent the wheel but can take a page from other sectors that are examining these issues as well.

Laurie Minott's article, "9 Proven Strategies to Improve Diversity, Equity & Inclusion at Your Workplace," provides a comprehensive list with explanations for each item, which I consider an excellent starting point:

1. Identify DEIB (Diversity, Equity, Inclusion & Belonging) as a strategic priority.

2. Conduct pay equity reviews.

3. Recruit and promote from a diverse point of view.

4. Create a robust mentorship program.

5. Consistently train and engage employees on DEIB.

6. Make sure benefits and programs are inclusive.

7. Set your ERGs (Employee Resource Groups) up for success.

8. Scrutinize board and executive team representation.

9. Make leaders accountable.[10]

The most difficult part of growth and change is the beginning. These are difficult topics and troubling times, but we have the opportunity to build something better than the society and systems we inherited.

---

10 Minott, Laurie. "9 Best Practices to Improve Diversity, Equity, and Inclusion." *Great Place to Work*, 22 June 2021, www.greatplacetowork.com/resources/blog/9-proven-strategies-to-improve-diversity-equity-inclusion-at-your-workplace.

Tech Leveling the Playing Field

Virtual learning is evolving as a new frontier of educational instruction. Specifically, I believe virtual learning holds promise for students with learning disabilities and the teachers who are in charge of their instruction. That's because virtual-learning environments encourage specialized supports and services that make for more tailored, differentiated instruction.

I've seen this work in practice. Teachers at Proximity Learning Inc. report that students with learning disabilities are able to perform at higher levels with online instruction because there are smaller class sizes, and students feel more empowered to engage and connect with their teachers.

The means by which we scaffold and differentiate instruction for students are designed to accommodate learners and their unique needs in classrooms that are committed to instruction in the least restrictive environment (LRE). Enhancing student learning is every educator's objective. For students with disabilities, a virtual or hybridized learning environment may offer robust, finely tuned instructional options. Of course, distracting events can still occur, but they are typically much more controlled than in a conventional setting. Based on my experience in the industry, many students with learning disabilities have trouble coping with sensory overstimulation. A virtual environment may provide them an opportunity to manage those stimuli and offer a means of mitigating distraction and engaging students in an enhanced-learning environment.

Teachers can design virtual instruction to focus on skill acquisition, including asking essential questions and analyzing micro and macro themes. Far too often, in my observation, instructional programming is teacher-centered. When done well, teachers can use virtual learning to maximize student-centered learning through specialized grouping, skill practice, and reflective thought that is leveraged and controlled through the technology architecture.

Finally, I believe that renewal in education should not be viewed through the lens of cynicism. Instead, it should be embraced as a means of reinvigorating our culture and the institution of education that reflects our nation's commitment to student achievement. Learning opportunities must advance, and we must embrace the future of our technology and America's ability to adapt reflexively to the needs of current and future generations.

Teachers do so much more than teach. Not just any person can be a teacher. While the old adage, "Those who can, do; those who can't, teach," still permeates many people's thoughts and views on teaching, the reality is most people cannot teach.

I hate this statement and it's a complete fallacy. It's been my experience that most people cannot simply fill the shoes of an expert teacher. They are intelligent, well educated, experienced, and trained professionals in their fields who are expected to shoulder the academic, social, and emotional well-being of young humans in the midst of chaos on strict and sometimes nonexistent budgets.

Consistently, I am thrilled, though not necessarily surprised, by how multitalented our teachers are. Those who can teach might very well be the modern-day version of the renaissance man or woman. Honestly, most teachers are multitalented individuals who can simply take their skill sets elsewhere and be treated more fairly with better pay, better hours, and more autonomy.

Teachers nurture creativity, critical thinking, and problem-solving skills, preparing individuals for the challenges of an ever-evolving world. Teachers provide a safe and supportive environment where students can express themselves, building confidence and self-esteem. Their impact transcends subject matter as they cultivate empathy, resilience, and social skills that empower students to navigate life's complexities and unexpected ups and downs. Teachers don't just impart knowledge, they shape the future by molding minds and hearts, leaving an indelible mark on generations to come.

Teachers shape not just minds but futures. Through their dedication, they sculpt the bridge between ignorance and enlightenment, nurturing the flames of curiosity in each student's heart. In classrooms, they are architects of potential, deserving of our utmost respect for their unwavering commitment to illuminating the path to knowledge.

> Let's abolish the old adage
> and trade it in for a new one:
> Those who can teach . . .
> are exceptional.

Keys to Solving the Education Crisis

Rebuilding our broken education system may seem like a lofty goal. But we are at the precipice of inspiration and transformation in not only the educational realm but also in the ways we move forward as a society. Whether people understand or believe it, teaching stands as the beacon that guides humanity forward. It's the only space that has the ability to bring together all types of individuals from all types of backgrounds and asks them to create a collective space. Through the sacred art of nurturing minds, it ignites the flames of progress, ensuring that wisdom and innovation flow ceaselessly from one generation to the next. In the tapestry of professions, teaching is the loom weaving the threads of possibility, making it the most important job in the world.

Teacher shortages, student social and emotional struggles, staggering achievement declines—where do we even begin? We have to start by respecting teachers and the profession. The lack of acknowledgment for their dedication creates a void that reverberates through the corridors of education. It's time for a movement, a resurgence of respect, to honor these guardians and bridge the gap between their unwavering commitment and society's appreciation. #TeachersServeToo

While there are no quick fixes, progress starts with communities united behind teachers and students. We all gain from strong public schools staffed by supported and certified professionals. Collaboration around tangible solutions is key. Recognizing the efforts of teachers goes beyond mere gestures; it requires a paradigm shift in societal perception towards education.

We need to truly listen to those on education's frontlines. Teachers, principals, counselors, support staff—their voices should lead the dialogue. They understand everyday realities and student needs. Top-down mandates by legislators or administrators fail because they lack classroom insights; they are typically only looking at one aspect of the education crisis, funding or lack thereof. Teachers are highly trained experts in their field, and it makes no sense that they are not part of the conversations or legislative processes when it comes to passing education legislation. We need a movement to restore respect for teachers; it's crucial to ensure the continuity of a robust educational system.

We truly need to invest in our existing teachers. Celebrating their dedication and achievements, instead of blaming them for the system's failures that were present well before they even began their first day of teaching, is critical. Leadership needs to make salaries competitive and restore respect to educators. We should make sure new and seasoned teachers are supported and provide mentorships, stipends for supplies, and opportunities for growth and professional development. Teachers need to have time to collaborate with one another and more autonomy and decision-making power when it comes to curriculum. There needs to be a way to reenergize the workforce by showing teachers their value and worth.

There also need to be significant improvements made to infrastructure. State and federal agencies need to fund improvements conveying education's value: modernize buildings, supply and improve technology, provide training, diverse classes, support staff, interventions, and enrichment programs. Leaders need to advocate for better pedagogy practices and doing what's best for students like implementing lower class sizes and student-counselor ratios or ceasing the reliance on myopic metrics like standardized tests. Let experienced teachers assess progress by measuring knowledge and skills rather than just test scores. Every single person in the education field should demonstrate a deep commitment to fully preparing our next generation.

Finally, there has to be an embrace of innovation that thoughtfully implements education technology to engage students and provide teacher flexibility. Blend digital tools with live teachers and supportive communities. By connecting virtual teachers to fill gaps, we provide the ability for personalized instruction and open access to electives.

Change takes time, but progress begins with one step. Schools flourish when teachers do. Students thrive when given support that meets their individual needs. By standing united behind public educational equity, we secure the future. Our nation prospers through knowledge, empathy, and unity—qualities teachers instill. We owe it to children to ensure every classroom has a caring, committed professional guiding their potential. The solutions exist if we listen and dedicate the will to act. #TeachersServeToo

Section Three

Effectiveness of
the Teacher

An effective teacher is more than a dispenser of information; he or she is a maestro of inspiration. Their presence radiates an aura of enthusiasm, an infectious passion that ignites the hearts of their students. Through a delicate dance of words, gestures, and expressions teachers are able to orchestrate an atmosphere of discovery, where every question is a gateway to understanding, and every mistake is a stepping stone to growth.

The teacher's effectiveness extends beyond the confines of textbooks. In the hands of an effective teacher, the classroom becomes a crucible of collaboration. Their skillful facilitation nurtures an environment where ideas flow freely and perspectives collide to create a symphony of learning. Students are not passive vessels but active participants in a grand dialogue, their voices amplified and validated by a teacher who recognizes the intrinsic value of every contribution.

Chapter Seven

It Starts at the Top:
Leader Effectiveness

As we look ahead into the next century,

leaders will be those who empower others.

Bill Gates

At the helm of educational institutions, effective leadership acts as both the architect and the catalyst for transformative change. Its impact ripples through the corridors of knowledge, empowering teachers with the tools to kindle curiosity and illuminate young minds. As this beacon of effective leadership shines, it fuels a virtuous cycle where motivated teachers fan the flames of passion within students, propelling them to rise as confident learners and future leaders themselves.

Most administrators will tell you they entered teaching without the plan to pivot into leadership, which sounds strange given that upward mobility in other industries means climbing the ladder and making the switch eventually to management and leadership roles. However, most teachers love the visible impact of their work in the classroom setting and want to stay in the classroom. Many school districts do not have a training program for future leaders. As a result, teachers are often promoted into this role without any real training. The people who end up in leadership positions have little to no experience as managers. Some certification programs for administrators require only a year or two of teaching in the classroom before they'll qualify an individual for a master's program/leadership certification program. So, how do we get school districts to emulate a well-run corporation by building a true leadership program that ensures people are provided the skills and coaching to succeed in their new roles? The turnover rate in school leadership positions is almost as high as teacher turnover. Leadership is not easy; going from a peer to a boss can be very taxing on a person mentally. Additionally, the key indicators of success (key performance indicators, KPI) change for their new role, They now might have to manage million-dollar budgets, hiring and firing, building maintenance, lawsuits, contracts, purchase decisions, etc. without any prior experience or training. Typically, in the corporate world you hire someone with experience in these roles, or you train someone to take over these responsibilities over multiple years as they grow into this position. Without the proper supports and training, it's no wonder so many leaders quit.

The Crucial Link Between Effective Leadership in Education and Student Success

In the realm of education, effective leadership acts as the cornerstone upon which schools, teachers, and students build a foundation for success. A dynamic leader can propel an educational institution from mediocrity to excellence and positively impact every facet of the learning environment.

Effective leadership in education goes beyond mere administrative duties; it embodies a visionary approach that aligns the school's mission with the needs and aspirations of its students. A great leader in education is one who fosters a culture of collaboration, continuous improvement, and innovation, steering the institution toward its goals while cultivating an environment that encourages exploration and growth.

The real magic in our field happens in the classroom, that interaction between teachers and students, that's where it all happens. I think there are many different layers that influence what happens in the classroom, but that is that point where the magic happens. As a school leader, as a principal, it was my job to make sure that teachers in my building had the conducive environment and culture in which to be able to work at their optimal levels. Teachers can't do their best work unless they have an environment and a culture that supports learning and supports them. That's the job of the administrator. And as a superintendent, it's my job to make sure that all teachers in all 39 schools that I have in my district, that they have the optimal level working conditions. And it's easy to say, it's not always easy to do, but that is the job to make sure that teachers have what they need and they're provided the space to be able to do their important work that they do every single day with kids.

Dr. Jermall Wright, superintendent
Little Rock School District

Supporting Schools through Strong Leadership

Strategic Planning. Effective leaders develop comprehensive strategies that encompass both short-term goals and long-term visions. They set clear objectives, allocate resources judiciously, and create a roadmap that enables the school to adapt and thrive in a rapidly changing educational landscape.

Cohesive Culture. A strong leader establishes a positive school culture that promotes open communication, shared values, and a sense of belonging among staff, students, and parents. This cohesive culture contributes to a harmonious learning environment where everyone is invested in the success of the institution.

Resource Management. Skillful leaders allocate resources effectively, ensuring that teachers have the tools, technology, and support needed to provide quality education. By making informed decisions about resource allocation, they create an environment where learning flourishes.

Empowering Teachers. Effective leadership plays a pivotal role in empowering teachers on their educational journey. By establishing a foundation of clear communication, professional development, and mutual respect, leadership creates a collaborative atmosphere where teachers feel valued and motivated. This empowerment goes beyond the classroom, as teachers equipped with the right guidance and resources can innovate and adapt their methods to address the evolving needs of students.

Professional Development. Effective leaders champion ongoing professional development for teachers. They recognize the value of nurturing educators' skills and knowledge, which in turn enhances teaching quality and student engagement.

Supportive Environment. A strong leader creates a supportive atmosphere in which teachers feel valued and empowered. This fosters a sense of ownership and dedication to their roles, ultimately translating to improved classroom experiences for students.

Collaboration. Leaders encourage collaboration among teachers, facilitating the exchange of best practices, ideas, and strategies. This collaborative spirit cultivates a culture of continuous learning and improvement.

Foundationally throughout my entire career as an educator, and as a superintendent, I have wholeheartedly believed that relationships are fundamental to achieving any goal—specifically academic goals and student achievement. I think it was Maya Angelo who said, people don't care about what you say, they care about how you make them feel. And my goal as an educator has always been to make sure that students feel like they are welcome and they belong.

Dr. Anna Stubblefield, superintendent of
Kansas City Public Schools

Sadly, leadership in education is not always so forgiving and supportive. Superintendents with perspectives like Dr. Stubblefield's serve as a stark contrast to the prevailing norms. In a landscape often marred by neglectful leadership, her approach stands as a rare gem. The unfortunate reality is that most leaders fall short in creating supportive environments due to a lack of training and support as they moved up in their careers. Instead of nurturing and empowering teachers, many administrators overlook the vital role relationships play in fostering a thriving educational community. It's imperative to reevaluate our educational paradigms and strive towards a future where principles of empowerment, collaboration, and a sense of belonging become the standard rather than the exception.

Collaboration, a cornerstone of progress, often takes a backseat, leaving classroom teachers isolated in their endeavors without the collective wisdom and collective support they desperately need in order to serve their students to the best of their ability.

Empowered Teachers Empower Students. Empowering teachers plays a pivotal role in fostering student success. When educators are provided with the tools, autonomy, and support to innovate and tailor their teaching methods to the diverse needs of their students, a positive ripple effect is created in the classroom.

> Empowered teachers illuminate the path of knowledge, guiding their students to reach heights they never thought possible.

Empowered teachers are more likely to develop engaging and interactive lessons, creating a dynamic learning environment that sparks curiosity and critical thinking. This, in turn, cultivates students' enthusiasm for learning, as they feel valued and understood. Furthermore, empowered teachers serve as role models, demonstrating the importance of lifelong learning and adaptability. Their enthusiasm and dedication inspire students to take ownership of their education, leading to improved academic performance, higher self-esteem, and a genuine passion for learning that extends beyond the classroom.

Student-Centric Approach. Effective leaders prioritize the needs of students above all else. They develop policies and initiatives that cater to diverse learning styles, abilities, and backgrounds, ensuring that each student receives a tailored education.

Safe and Inclusive Environment. A skillful leader creates an environment where students feel safe, respected, and valued. This inclusivity fosters a positive mindset and encourages active participation in the learning process.

High Expectations. Effective leaders set high expectations for both teachers and students, inspiring them to aim for excellence. By nurturing a growth mindset, they encourage students to strive for their best and continuously challenge themselves.

In the intricate tapestry of education, effective leadership is the thread that weaves together schools, teachers, and students into a cohesive and thriving community. A visionary leader guides institutions toward success, empowering teachers to excel and nurturing an environment in which students can thrive. The impact of effective leadership in education reverberates far beyond administrative duties; it shapes the very trajectory of society by producing capable, engaged, and inspired individuals ready to shape the world.

Demanding Exceptional Leadership in Education. Quality classrooms are not solely the result of exceptional teachers and engaged students; rather, they begin at the top, with effective campus leadership. The role of school administrators and campus leaders cannot be overstated when it comes to creating an environment that nurtures academic excellence, fosters a positive culture, and supports the growth of both educators and students. A strong and visionary leadership team sets the tone for the entire educational institution by influencing policies, instructional practices, and the overall learning experience. Through their strategic decisions, unwavering commitment to educational goals, and genuine concern for the well-being of all stakeholders effective campus leaders lay the foundation for a thriving educational community where every classroom can flourish.

Servant Leadership in Every Institution

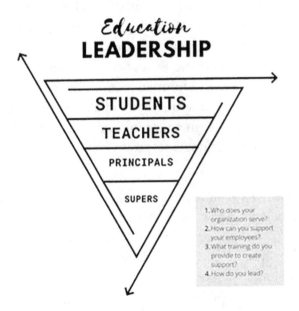

Servant leadership felt impossible for me to achieve as I built Proximity Learning. Around every corner was a new challenge and every reason to ignore it and just forge ahead. However, making servant leadership a priority has allowed me to build trust with my team and create an open environment where everyone feels heard and important. From my experience, being thoughtful about focusing on the needs of others can help:

- Naturally build stronger relationships with your team
- Earn their trust and respect
- Inspire them to work harder and achieve more

This infographic did a great job for my leadership team when we were building out the type of structure we wanted at our company. The flow of focus goes from customers to employees to management to President. By making a commitment to serving others, you and your team will unlock a powerful leadership style that can transform your organization.

Utilizing a servant leadership approach within the realm of education has the potential to yield substantial benefits. This methodology places emphasis on fostering a nurturing and empowering environment, where educators focus on serving the needs of their students, colleagues, and the educational community at large. By embracing servant leadership in education, educators can cultivate a culture of collaboration, empathy, and shared growth, ultimately leading to enhanced student engagement, holistic development, and a more harmonious learning ecosystem.

> *I always say I would never ask a staff member to do something that I would not personally do. Now I may not have the expertise to do it, but I would be willing to learn to do it. And I've done everything from help the custodians clean up an area to help people set up for an event.*
>
> Dr. Anna Stubblefield, superintendent of
> Kansas City Public Schools

Strong Leadership Attracts the Best Candidates

In today's competitive job market, it is essential to have employees who possess the skills to thrive alongside rapid technological advancements, evolving customer preferences, and industry uncertainties.

As an industry leader, one of my top priorities is to attract the candidates who fit best with my team, clients, and vision. While education and experience are critically important, over the last few years, my company's hiring team has focused on revealing which potential candidates will be most durable.

Durable Versus Perishable Skills

Durable skills include a combination of how a person uses what they know in life and how they are able to apply this knowledge in the workplace. Durable skills encompass critical thinking, communication, collaboration, and creativity, as well as character skills such as fortitude, growth mindset, and leadership. A study across 80 million job postings found these skills to be the ones most in demand.

Unlike perishable skills, durable skills are considered nonstatic as they develop over time and can be used in any industry or work environment.

Attraction and Development of Durable Skills

With demand high for these types of skills, to attract workers who possess durable skills, I believe we need to create a workplace culture that values and fosters continuous learning and development. One way to achieve this is obviously by offering competitive compensation and benefits packages.

More importantly, though, is screening for things like critical thinking skills, the ability to communicate effectively with others, and a growth mindset. These are just a few of those durable skills that I think a company should highlight in a candidate's application.

Culture Index Diagnostic Tool

Another great way to make sure leadership is attracting good fits for the team is using screening tools that measure these types of skills. My company uses a culture index diagnostic tool. This provides us with a "cheat sheet" that identifies how different people are built to perform, which enables our leadership team to identify the key traits we believe will make a person successful in a role. We then match the candidates to these positions so that they have the best chance to succeed.

I recommend putting together an index based on the criteria most important to your company and its various roles. I've found this tool extremely useful in helping put together leadership teams and identifying strengths, opportunities for growth, and development of durable skills. However, attracting workers with durable skills is only one part of the solution.

In-House Training and Team Building

In addition to attracting the right people with these skill sets, there also needs to be in-house opportunities for developing durable skills such as leadership and development programs, mentorship programs, and on-the-job training.

Organization leaders have to ensure current employees have the opportunity to develop these skills in-house. One way to achieve this is by offering continuous professional-development opportunities. This can include online courses and workshops.

There should also be ample organizational relationship/ team-building opportunities. As an example, my company recently instituted a VTO or paid volunteer time off benefit. Employees receive an additional five paid days off to specifically volunteer in their communities, individually or with their teams. I see this as a way to connect with our community and create learning opportunities for our employees outside the company. Monthly, we highlight one employee's VTO experience to motivate employees to make use of the policy.

Durable Skills and Company Culture

We also need to be inclusive and encouraging about learning and refining durable skills within the organization. This means creating an environment where employees feel comfortable taking risks and making mistakes, as long as they learn from them. They also need to feel like they can ask questions honestly; it's all about creating an environment that fosters support.

As leaders, we can make this easier by sharing and celebrating successes, providing constructive feedback, and recognizing employees who take initiative and are committed to continuous improvement.

> *It's extremely important that time is spent with the Board of Education and the superintendent discussing what is the real root of the issue and what are the problems we're really trying to solve, and taking the time to study, look at the best available research that's available, communicating to the public what we're about to do, and helping them understand why changes need to happen and what those changes will look like.*
>
> Dr. Shawn Joseph, Assistant Professor/
> Co-Director of Urban Superintendent
> Academy, Howard University

Moreover, organizations need to align training and development programs with the skills needed to succeed in the future. This means identifying the skills that will be in high demand and providing our employees with the necessary training and development opportunities to acquire them.

Attracting workers with durable skills and helping current employees develop these skills in-house are essential for any organization's long-term success. As a leader, it is our responsibility to create a workplace culture that values continuous learning and development, offers growth opportunities, and aligns programming with the skills needed to succeed in the future.

Chapter Eight

Strategic Remembering, Engagement, and Relationship Building

None of us got where we are solely by pulling ourselves up by our bootstraps. We got here because somebody—a parent, a teacher, an Ivy League crony or a few nuns—bent down and helped us pick up our boots.

Thurgood Marshall

In any classroom, three crucial elements stand out as the pillars of success: Strategic Remembering, Engagement, and Building Relationships. As technology continues to shape the educational landscape, teachers play an indispensable role in leveraging these key aspects to create a meaningful and enriching learning experience for their students. Strategic Remembering involves employing innovative methods to enhance retention and application of knowledge, fostering a deeper understanding of the subject matter. Engagement entails capturing students' attention and maintaining their active involvement through interactive and immersive learning activities. Building Relationships, though challenging in the virtual realm, is vital for establishing a supportive and inclusive classroom community. Teachers—with their expertise, adaptability, and dedication—are the driving force behind the implementation of these principles, ultimately shaping the path to success in the virtual classroom and beyond.

This chapter is all about creating an effective approach to teaching in the twenty-first-century classroom. We will cover the top three strategies for maximizing outcomes.

Strategic Remembering: Elevating the Learning Experience

Have you ever read a powerful book and a year later remembered only a few words of it? Your brain is like a hard drive, the space is limited. It protects you from overloading on information, so new data is stored in the short-term memory, not long-term memory. If we don't reinforce, repeat, and use things right away, new ideas go into our short-term memory and never make it into our long-term memory. Hermann Ebbinghaus describes that after one hour of learning something new, we forget more than 50 percent of the information. One day later, we remember just 30 percent. However, through constant repetition, you can take a concept from short-term memory and move it to long-term memory and eventually turn it into a habit.

In the digital age, Strategic Remembering becomes a dynamic tool for educators. Virtual classrooms offer an array of technological possibilities, and teachers can harness this potential to enhance students' retention and application of knowledge. From interactive online quizzes to engaging multimedia resources, educators employ innovative methods to ensure that students not only remember what they learn but also deeply understand it.

Engagement:
The Power of Active Participation

Engagement is the heartbeat of the classroom. It's not enough to passively watch lectures and read materials; true learning occurs when students actively participate and immerse themselves in the learning process. Engagement fosters curiosity, critical thinking, and a deeper understanding of the subject matter.

One of the most amazing things I've been able to see in Proximity Learning's digital classroom is the ability of teachers to take students beyond the walls of their classrooms. These highly-qualified online teachers stop at nothing to make the experiences rich, rewarding, and educational. With the right technology, tools, and training, online learning can be more than just a crutch for educators. We can use it to bring equitable education to students everywhere. Here are a few strategies we have learned and implement in our classrooms to drive engagement:

Interactive Tools. Utilize the interactive features of virtual classrooms. Chat functions, polls, and breakout rooms can transform passive listeners into active participants, encouraging discussions and questions.

Real-World Application. Connect lessons to real-life scenarios to make the content more relatable and engaging. Encourage students to apply what they learn to their own experiences.

Group Projects. Collaborative assignments and group projects encourage teamwork and active engagement. They also provide opportunity for students to teach and learn from their peers.

Instructor Feedback. Constructive feedback from instructors plays a pivotal role in student engagement. It acknowledges effort and guides improvement.

Gamification. Introduce gamified elements into the learning process to make it more enjoyable and competitive, fostering a spirit of healthy engagement.

Building Relationships:
The Glue that Bonds the Virtual Classroom

In the virtual classroom, students and educators are not physically present in the same space. However, the power of connection transcends physical boundaries. Building Relationships is the third pillar of success, creating an environment of trust, support, and collaboration.

Emotional Support. A sense of belonging and emotional support is crucial, especially in virtual settings. Educators can create a safe space for students to express themselves and ask questions without fear.

Peer Networks. Encourage students to connect with their peers. Virtual classrooms provide opportunities for diverse interactions and the exchange of ideas from around the world.

Instructor-Student Bond. Building a strong bond between instructors and students is vital. This rapport fosters open communication, making it easier for students to seek guidance and assistance.

Mentorship. Encourage mentorship programs where more experienced students can guide newcomers. This not only aids in academic growth but also strengthens the sense of community.

The Students Are NOT Okay:
The Impact of SEL on Education

Any educator can tell you that we aren't seeing a staggering academic achievement gap growing. Social and emotional learning gaps are also at the nexus of the teacher-transitioning-out-of-the-classroom movement. Across the country educators are reporting a deluge of mental health and social/emotional issues being played out on their campuses and in the classrooms. Students have had a difficult time simply learning how to "do school" again. We have to create safe, emotionally-supportive environments with live teachers who can meet the students "where they are," before we can even begin to close those learning gaps. Students learn best when their basic, social, and emotional needs are being met first.

Social and Emotional Learning (SEL) has emerged as a powerful educational approach that goes beyond academic achievement by focusing on the holistic development of students. By cultivating self-awareness, empathy, and responsible decision-making, SEL equips students with essential life skills that contribute to their personal growth, well-being, and success in all areas of life. As educators continue to recognize the importance of nurturing emotional intelligence, the incorporation of SEL in the classroom will undoubtedly play a vital role in shaping a more compassionate, resilient, and inclusive society.

In recent years, educators and researchers have recognized the significance of nurturing not only students' academic skills but also their social and emotional development. SEL has emerged as a critical approach in modern education, with its focus on equipping students with essential life skills, emotional intelligence, and interpersonal abilities. By incorporating SEL in the classroom, educators can create a supportive environment that empowers students to navigate challenges, build healthy relationships, and thrive both academically and personally.

What Is SEL?

Social and Emotional Learning is an educational framework that emphasizes the development of essential life skills in students. It encompasses a broad range of competencies, including self-awareness, self-management, social awareness, relationship skills, and responsible decision-making. SEL recognizes that emotional well-being and interpersonal competence are crucial not only for academic success, but also for fostering a positive and inclusive school climate.

The Core Competencies of SEL

Self-Awareness. This involves recognizing and understanding one's emotions, strengths, weaknesses, and values. Self-aware students are better equipped to manage their feelings and behaviors effectively.

Self-Management. The ability to regulate emotions, set goals, and persevere in the face of challenges is crucial for personal growth and academic achievement.

Social Awareness. Empathy and understanding the feelings, needs, and perspectives of others are at the core of social awareness. It fosters compassion and a sense of community in the classroom.

Relationship Skills. Developing healthy relationships is vital for collaboration and effective communication. SEL helps students build and maintain positive connections with peers and teachers.

Responsible Decision-Making. Teaching students to make ethical and informed choices empowers them to navigate complex situations and resolve conflicts constructively.

The Importance of SEL in the Classroom

Academic Success. Research shows that students who participate in SEL programs tend to exhibit improved academic performance. By addressing emotional barriers to learning, SEL helps students engage more effectively with their studies.

Positive Behavior and Classroom Climate. SEL cultivates a sense of trust and respect among students and between students and teachers. A positive classroom climate fosters a supportive learning environment where everyone feels valued and safe.

Emotional Regulation. In the face of stress and adversity, students equipped with SEL skills can manage their emotions better, reducing disruptive behaviors and promoting a focused-learning atmosphere.

Conflict Resolution. SEL teaches students how to resolve conflicts peacefully, which contributes to a harmonious classroom atmosphere and reduces instances of bullying and aggression.

Long-Term Well-being. The emotional intelligence cultivated through SEL has long-lasting effects beyond the classroom. Students who develop strong SEL skills are more likely to lead fulfilling and successful lives as adults.

Implementing SEL in the Classroom

Teacher Training. Before integrating SEL into their classrooms, teachers should receive appropriate training and support. Understanding the principles of SEL and its implementation strategies is crucial for its effective delivery.

Curriculum Integration. SEL can be infused into various aspects of the curriculum, such as through literature discussions, group projects, and problem-solving activities. Infusing SEL into daily lessons ensures it becomes an integral part of students' learning experience.

Classroom Practices. Teachers can incorporate activities that promote self-awareness, empathy, and collaboration. Activities like journaling, role-playing, and group discussions provide opportunities for students to develop their social and emotional skills.

Parent/Family Involvement. Encouraging parental involvement in SEL initiatives can reinforce the development of these skills outside the classroom and create a cohesive approach to fostering emotional intelligence.

Putting It All Together

To succeed in this new era of learning, one must master the Three Pillars of Success: Strategic Remembering, Engagement, and Building Relationships. These pillars serve as a roadmap, guiding both educators and learners towards the realization of their educational goals in the limitless world of learning. By embracing these principles, we can unlock the full potential of the classroom and make learning an enriching and transformative experience.

I hate the saying, "Those who can, do, and those who can't, teach." This is one of the biggest misconceptions about the teaching profession and denigrates the profession and teachers in general.

It's been my experience that most people cannot simply fill the shoes of an expert teacher. Consistently, I am blown away by how multitalented our teachers are. Having a heart-to-heart conversation and discovering that so many teachers are not only experts in their fields of study but also seem to embody the renaissance man or woman, completely contradicts the portrayal of teachers in popular culture.

Some of these individuals are also performing musicians, business owners, run nonprofits, sing in local or church choirs, write and publish books, and even worked at big tech companies, while teaching full time!

Honestly, most teachers are multitalented individuals who can simply take their skill sets elsewhere and be treated more fairly with better pay, better hours, and more autonomy. If we hope to attract and retain top talent in the teaching profession, we have to abolish that old adage and trade it in for a new one: Those who can teach . . . are exceptional! And we should treat them no less than such.

Section Four

Global Impact of the Virtual World

From the vast tapestry of creativity came endless possibilities in the digital dawn. Once a whisper, the virtual world now towers over communication, connection, and human experience worldwide. The effect of the virtual world can't be ignored anymore!

The initial threads of this virtual tapestry created change in society in ways never before seen. People from different parts of the world were connected by the invisible threads of the digital web, making geographic distances irrelevant. Virtual symphonies blurred borders, cultures clashed, and languages harmonized.

In this networked world, thoughts are no longer limited to university halls and intellectual groups. Anyone with a voice and screen can contribute to global dialogue. A small-village adolescent might speak about climate change to the world. A young artist can reach an audience outside galleries.

The worldwide significance of the virtual world is still being written on future blank pages. Its progress depends on digital and physical users' choices. It challenges civilization to rethink community, identity, and connection. It urges people to carefully use the virtual environment to promote growth, inclusivity, and positive change. And, perhaps most importantly, it raises questions surrounding hiring, governance, and ethical considerations.

The #TeachersServeToo movement, with its advocacy for recognizing the multifaceted roles of educators, intertwines seamlessly with the global impact of the virtual world. As the digital dawn envelops communication and human experience, it not only erases geographical boundaries but also redefines the essence of global connectivity. The virtual tapestry weaves stories of inclusivity, where voices once confined to specific spaces now resonate worldwide. This interconnectedness underscores the significance of hiring strategies in the evolving educational landscape. In a world where hiring extends beyond local limitations, districts can tap into a diverse pool of educators, transcending borders to recruit exceptional teachers. This shift reshapes the educational paradigm, offering students access to specialized courses and expertise previously limited by geographical constraints.

Chapter Nine

Hiring

"From 'crisis' to 'catastrophe,' schools scramble once again to find teachers."

NBC News, August 13, 2023, Shannon Pettypiece

As education evolves to embrace virtual classrooms, the significance of hiring strategies tailored to this dynamic environment becomes increasingly evident. At the heart of these strategies lies the paramount importance of valuing and attracting high-quality teachers. Selecting educators who possess the expertise, adaptability, and passion to thrive in the classroom realm is pivotal to fostering a successful and enriching learning experience for students. The twenty-first-century classroom demands unique skills, including tech-savviness, strong communication abilities, and innovative teaching approaches, making the recruitment process a critical determinant to the overall success of education. By prioritizing the selection of exceptional educators, educational institutions can ensure a supportive and engaging learning environment that equips students with the knowledge and skills necessary to thrive in an ever-changing world.

The growing focus on virtual schools hiring virtual teachers marks a remarkable shift in the educational landscape. Gone are the days when districts were constrained to their immediate geographical applicant pools. Now they possess the ability to cast a wider net, potentially recruiting educators from across the state, the nation, or even beyond borders. While credentialing requirements such as a bachelor's degree and state certification remain essential for quality assurance, this newfound flexibility empowers districts to offer a diverse array of subjects that might have been previously unavailable due to a lack of local expertise. Think Mandarin Chinese or AP statistics; now, students can access these specialized courses, led by highly qualified teachers who may reside thousands of miles away, but who can provide a world-class education without geographical constraints. This newfound accessibility broadens educational horizons and enriches the learning experiences for students everywhere.

Inflation and the Teacher Shortage

If you've scrolled through LinkedIn recently, you may have noticed the hashtag #teachertransition has been gaining traction and shows no signs of slowing down.

While it's no secret the teacher shortage was exacerbated by the pandemic—and many districts have been in a tailspin to retain their current teachers as they try to hire replacement teachers to fill vacancies—one cannot help but wonder: Is there any hope for public education on the horizon as the country watches the cost of everything soar?

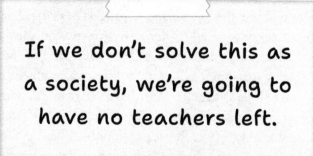

If we don't solve this as a society, we're going to have no teachers left.

It's a daunting reality. But a recent *Wall Street Journal* article said that among public schools, 44 percent reported full- or part-time teaching vacancies at the start of the year.[11] This is insanity. And you know, the transitioning teachers are NOT to blame. The system has failed them and the students. It was failing for decades prior to this mass exodus. We really need to be looking at building something better rather than saving an institutionalized education system that is clearly failing. Let's stop dreaming and start building.

A massive exodus of 2.6 million US educators and staff quit public K–12 and higher education jobs during the pandemic, and the departures continue. But can more money solve the shortage and the debilitating systemic issues faced by schools nationwide?

Increasing teachers' salaries has done little to slow the ever-growing vacancies amidst one of the worst inflated economies since the early 2000's recession. Despite the average teacher salary going up to approximately $66,000 nationwide in 2023, the wage increases cannot keep pace with rising gas prices, exorbitant rental and real estate bubbles, grocery bills, childcare costs, etc. Salary increases and sign-on bonuses can't combat the rising cost of living.

When I started teaching in 1997, it just seemed like there was always something else to do or there was some facet of my job that I didn't know and had to learn.

There was so much that I had to do besides just opening up a book and teaching. Fast forward to 2023, man, the demands of teachers have skyrocketed since my time in the classroom and sometimes it's hard to imagine it getting any more difficult. So number two I would say is understanding what teachers have to go through.

Dr. Jermall Wright, superintendent
Little Rock School District

---

11 Dill, Kathryn. "School's Out for Summer and Many Teachers Are Calling It Quits." *WSJ*, www.wsj.com/articles/schools-out-for-summer-and-many-teachers-are-calling-it-quits-11655732689.

As the founder of a digital education provider, I believe $200 billion in federal funding should have been more than enough to stop the hemorrhage—but where did it go? Federal relief funds for school districts range anywhere from $5000 to $20,000 per student. But that money isn't necessarily going toward hiring new teachers or helping students catch up. Facility upgrades, pandemic health supplies, and fighting 8 percent inflation all play a role.

In some cases, the states withheld their normal funding and told schools to use the available federal funding instead. The reality is that teachers cannot expect to see a significant improvement in pay or help from the federal relief funds. We have to continue to push for alternatives, like live virtual learning, to solve long-term problems.

I think there must be better incentives, and we have to level the playing field for our educators if we want to keep them in the industry. We cannot expect these highly educated, trained, and experienced individuals to continue to work above and beyond their pay scale while never recouping the costs.

The Wage Penalty for Teachers

According to Emily Tate's article, "We All Know Teachers Are Underpaid. But Who Imagined It Was This Bad?," teachers are some of the most underpaid for their education and experience levels in the nation. For example, she states that one recent study "controlled for levels of education and years of experience" reported teachers "make less money on the dollar than their peers in comparable fields, a concept known as the wage penalty."[12]

To further prove her point, she brings up data from The Economic Policy Institute, which found "that public school teachers nationally make about 19 percent less than employees in commensurate professions, or about 81 cents on the dollar." According to the

12 Tate, Emily, et al. "We All Know Teachers Are Underpaid. But Who Imagined It Was This Bad?" *Mother Jones*, 30 Mar. 2022, www.motherjones.com/politics/2022/03/we-all-know-teachers-are-underpaid-but-who-imagined-it-was-this-bad.

data, the wage penalty has increased significantly, compared to only 6 percent in 1996.[13]

We can't expect teachers to take on multiple responsibilities and roles in the classroom and still struggle to make ends meet. Neither should there be an expectation that they must moonlight or take on multiple side gigs, as Tate's article points out.

I believe educators should be valued for their education and work experience and should have a fair chance at advancement in their chosen field. The status quo notion that teachers should continue to go on underpaid speaks volumes about how we, as a society, value not only our teachers but also our student populations.

I don't think we can solve the problem if we don't talk about it or ignore the staggering data—we are setting up generations of students to struggle and fail.

A Potential Solution: Virtual Education Options

Digital education providers can step in to address the gaps caused by teacher shortages. To attract new talent effectively, it's crucial to offer competitive packages that encompass not only compensation but also flexible scheduling and the possibility of working from home or in a hybrid model. The reality is that in the realm of virtual education, these opportunities are readily available.

What's interesting is that I've observed a positive trend among online education providers. When educators are provided with choices and options, it tends to lead to improved hiring rates and increased teacher satisfaction. It's worth noting that some of these providers were already making these strides even before the onset of the pandemic.

Support and training are absolutely essential when helping teachers make the transition from traditional classrooms to virtual

---

13 Tate, Emily, et al. "We All Know Teachers Are Underpaid. But Who Imagined It Was This Bad?" *Mother Jones*, 30 Mar. 2022, www.motherjones.com/politics/2022/03/we-all-know-teachers-are-underpaid-but-who-imagined-it-was-this-bad.

teaching environments. Therefore, education technology providers must acknowledge the distinct challenges these teachers will encounter and provide them with the time and resources they need to grow. Collaborating with virtual-learning associations and providers can play a pivotal role in assisting new virtual classroom teachers in adapting to this landscape.

If we're aiming for a brighter future for our students, we must first create a better present for our teachers. As we approach another year grappling with achievement gaps and students requiring not only academic assistance but also increased social and emotional support, it's crucial to be honest about the challenges facing our schools, students, teachers, and communities.

Transitioning Traditional Teachers to the Virtual Classroom

Imagine a seasoned teacher who's spent years in the bustling world of traditional classrooms who suddenly finds him- or herself navigating the virtual teaching frontier. It's like switching from a well-worn hiking trail to a high-tech, augmented-reality adventure. The terrain is different, the tools are new, and the rules have changed. But fear not, because in this digital age, transitioning traditional teachers to the virtual classroom is not just a challenge but an opportunity to harness the power of technology and adapt teaching methods for a new generation of learners. In this exploration, we'll uncover the key steps, strategies, and insights to make this transition smoother than ever before.

Empowering former teachers to pivot into a new classroom environment may seem daunting at first, but with the right support, training, and growth mindset, teachers can lead successful virtual classes and become some of your most valuable employees.

Look for Transferable Skills

Transitioning from a traditional classroom to a virtual one may seem like a leap, but rest assured, teachers are not starting from scratch.

Many of the skills they've cultivated in traditional teaching can be seamlessly transferred to the virtual classroom. First and foremost, their ability to create engaging lesson plans and convey complex concepts is invaluable regardless of the setting. Moreover, classroom management skills— including maintaining a structured and inclusive learning environment—still apply, albeit with some digital adjustments. Their knack for adapting to diverse student needs and providing constructive feedback remains as essential as ever in the virtual realm. Additionally, their communication skills, both verbal and written, will prove vital for clear online instruction and correspondence. Last, empathy and patience, qualities that make a great teacher, are universal and will continue to shape a teacher's success in the virtual classroom. So take comfort in knowing that while the scenery may change, teaching skills remain a sturdy foundation for this new educational frontier.

A Comprehensive Onboarding Process

Imagine embarking on a virtual teaching adventure with all the tools, knowledge, and support you need right from the start. That's the magic of a robust onboarding process. It's like having a trusty map and a seasoned guide as you venture into the digital classroom. This process should be a warm welcome, offering a detailed tour of the virtual landscape, from the technology they'll be using to the teaching methodologies that work best online. It's a chance to connect with fellow educators, share insights, and feel like part of a team, even if they're miles apart. And don't forget the lifelines: readily available tech support, resources, and training to keep your journey smooth. A solid onboarding system is your ticket to a confident and successful start in this exciting educational realm!

Providing Leadership Opportunities to Virtual Teachers

In the world of virtual classrooms, teachers play a pivotal role, but they often have limited leadership opportunities. However, it's essential to recognize that teachers possess valuable insights and experiences that can drive improvements in online education. By giving them more leadership responsibilities, we're harnessing their expertise to make virtual learning more effective and engaging. Teachers can contribute significantly to shaping the virtual classroom experience, making it more tailored to the needs of both educators and students. Providing more leadership opportunities to teachers in the virtual classroom isn't just a smart move, it's a way to enhance the quality of online education.

Focus on Upskilling and Reskilling

As education journeys into the virtual realm, the role of teachers is evolving faster than ever. That's where upskilling and reskilling come into play. It's like giving our teachers a toolkit filled with new skills and techniques to thrive in this digital landscape. Just as a seasoned traveler learns the local language, teachers too need to master the language of virtual teaching. This means getting comfortable with new tech tools, refining online communication skills, and exploring innovative teaching methods that keep students engaged from behind the screen. Upskilling and reskilling aren't just about adapting, they're about flourishing. So, let's equip our educators with the tools they need to not only navigate but to excel in the virtual classroom, ensuring that every student's educational journey continues to be insightful and impactful.

Online learning platforms like FutureLearn, Coursera, LinkedIn Learning, Verb, and edX are excellent examples of tools that can help with upskilling and reskilling. We recently began using one of these platforms and are seeing excellent strides with leadership development to help both existing team members and new ones cultivate their skills.

Tech and Filling Teacher Vacancies

As of June 2022, The *Wall Street Journal's* Kathryn Dill reported that "Some 300,000 public-school teachers and other staff left the field between February 2020 and May 2022, a nearly 3 percent drop in that workforce, according to Bureau of Labor Statistics data."

Reports like the recent National Education Association's poll conducted this year finding that 55 percent of teachers said they would leave education sooner than planned.[14] The education sector is desperate to fill vacant positions and welcome students back this fall without having to resort to substitute teacher coverage (another subgroup that's experiencing massive shortages as well).

Each vacant teaching position represents a missed opportunity to provide students with the high-quality education they deserve. The impact of such vacancies reverberates for years, influencing educational outcomes significantly. Extensive research has illuminated the dire consequences of teacher absences on students. When educational institutions face challenges in filling critical positions, such as math and English, it directly correlates with declines in test scores and learning achievements, as evidenced by reductions in standard deviations.

A recent article by Desiree Carver-Thomas for the Learning Policy Institute pointed out that "teacher shortages can significantly depress student achievement, as schools often cancel courses due to vacancies or staff classes with substitutes and under-prepared teachers who are not certified to teach their subject matter."

Some states like California and Connecticut have responded to shortages by reducing the qualifications and certifications to enter the classroom, but this undermines students' opportunities to learn from expert teachers, which especially impacts students of color and those in economically disadvantaged areas.

Having a "warm body" in classrooms doesn't guarantee effective learning or sustainable educational solutions. Research indicates that novice or ill-prepared teachers tend to leave their positions at rates two to three times higher than those who enter with

14 Walker, Tim. "Survey: Alarming Number of Educators May Soon Leave the Profession | NEA." *Survey: Alarming Number of Educators May Soon Leave the Profession | NEA*, 1 Feb. 2022, www.nea.org/nea-today/all-news-articles/survey-alarming-number-educators-may-soon-leave-profession.

comprehensive training.[15] This teacher turnover creates instability, affecting both students and educators.

However, the solution doesn't involve lowering the standards and recruiting anyone willing to take on the role. The truth is that we're in a race against time to address the teacher shortage crisis, with school and district positions remaining unfilled at record levels. Yet, despite the challenges of another school year marked by significant losses and missed opportunities, administrators and districts still have viable options at their disposal.

Leveraging technology is a smart move in our mission to combat the teacher shortage. It's like having a versatile tool that can help fill the educational gaps. With the right tech in place, we can expand the reach of expert educators through virtual classrooms. This means that a talented teacher in one location can teach students from different parts of the world, bridging geographical barriers. Additionally, educational technology can assist in automating administrative tasks, freeing up educators' time to focus on teaching. Moreover, AI-powered tools can provide personalized learning experiences, cater to individual student needs, and reduce the burden on teachers. Technology isn't just a solution, it's a key ally in addressing the teacher shortage while enhancing the quality of education for students.

Technology as a Solution

In the voices of my virtual instructors, I witnessed a powerful transformation echoed across the educational landscape. Their transition to online teaching unlocked a profound sense of autonomy and a reclaimed ownership of their time. As educators navigated the digital realm, they discovered newfound flexibility in crafting lessons, connecting with students, and balancing personal and professional commitments.

15 Sorensen, Lucy C., and Helen F. Ladd. "The Hidden Costs of Teacher Turnover." *AERA Open*, vol. 6, no. 1, SAGE Publications, Jan. 2020, p. 233285842090581. *Crossref*, doi:10.1177/2332858420905812.

This paradigm shift isn't merely about adapting to technology, it's a testament to the concept of the #TeachersServeToo movement. It begins with recognizing the invaluable dedication of educators and empowering them with the tools and environment that honor their expertise while preserving their well-being. It's about recognizing their status and backgrounds as professionals in their industries and trusting them to be the amazing classroom leaders they are.

These are modern times, and there are modern solutions that can bring education out of the dark ages and into the twenty-first century. While virtual learning has gotten a bad rap these last few years because of the pandemic scramble to launch virtual classrooms across the nation by unprepared (and untrained) districts, teachers, and students, virtual learning can be the saving grace to fill teacher vacancies.

Here's what did not work during the pandemic: moving traditional curriculum onto a Zoom call isn't an effective virtual-learning approach. From my perspective as a digital education entrepreneur, this is where many school districts struggled most. Most districts have attempted to take a curriculum developed for asynchronous learning (i.e., the click, click, next solution) and try to repurpose it for true virtual instruction, rather than investing in a dynamic online curriculum. Students are not going to log in, turn on their cameras or engage with content or teachers they cannot personally connect to.

I am a firm believer that nothing replaces a well-qualified and credentialed teacher, and we can bring those live, expert teachers to students and districts regardless of geographic location. Live virtual teaching allows schools to draw from a national pool of qualified candidates. It's been my passion and mission to introduce districts and administrators to stellar teams of teachers who just happen to be virtual educators—that's literally what I do.

The technology is actually much simpler than it seems. By livestreaming teachers into classrooms or student homes, we do two things: eliminate the geographic barrier to finding educators within a given location and provide teachers the flexibility and working conditions they need and deserve.

Therefore, instead of being limited to the area around them, districts can choose teachers with expertise outside the schools' usual core curriculum, giving students expanded access to elective and enrichment courses for all grade levels.

And administrators and districts can choose to keep schools open, providing access to services and supervision while they receive live virtual teaching from credentialed, experienced, expert teachers. This technology doesn't replace teachers or brick-and-mortar schools, it adds flexibility as well as viable quality education options and alternatives for an otherwise hobbled industry.

Regardless of whether remote learning is taking place in the household or in the brick-and-mortar schools, parents, administrators, and students know they are receiving a quality education. Technology and flexibility can go a long way toward relieving the limited teacher supply, and we have to get ahead of the limitations that have been set upon the education system in the past.

We have to move forward. We have to do better. And we don't have to reinvent the wheel. We have all the tools and technology we need at our fingertips right now to support struggling schools and districts. With the right virtual-learning technology implementation, schools don't have to dread their local teacher shortages. In this modern age, quality education and live expert teachers are just a click away.

Chapter Ten

Governance

I am not bound to win, but I am bound to be true. I am not bound to succeed, but I am bound to live by the light that I have. I must stand with anybody that stands right, and stand with him while he is right, and part with him when he goes wrong.

Abraham Lincoln

The intricate web of educational policy, state laws, and local governance intersects profoundly with the #TeachersServeToo movement, spotlighting the pivotal role these structures play in sculpting the classroom landscape. These governing frameworks serve as the blueprint for deploying and managing both in-person and virtual-learning environments, thereby wielding significant influence over educators' and students' experiences. From budgetary allocations, to curriculum frameworks, and professional development initiatives, decisions at the policy level bear immense weight on the efficacy and inclusivity of virtual education. At the core of this lies the pursuit of equitable access to technology, connectivity, and support services, all pivotal in enabling teachers to craft engaging, impactful lessons for diverse student cohorts. Acknowledging the impact of educational policies and local regulations on virtual education stands as a cornerstone for empowering teachers to adeptly navigate this dynamic sphere, ensuring an optimal learning journey for their students as advocated in #TeachersServeToo.

The Crucial Role of Governance

When we talk about governance in education, we're referring to all the decisions and policies that basically set the stage for how learning happens. And let me tell you, these decisions have a big impact on both teachers and students, shaping the whole education experience. It's like they're the architects of this new way of learning!

Education is not an isolated endeavor; it's a complex ecosystem where governance serves as the backbone. From funding and resource allocation to curriculum design and teacher training, decisions made at the policy level have far-reaching consequences. These decisions can either unlock the full potential of virtual education or create barriers that hinder its effectiveness and accessibility.

Equity in Virtual Education

At the heart of governance in virtual education is the concept of equity. Ensuring equitable access to technology, reliable internet connectivity, and support services is paramount. These factors are not mere luxuries; they are the lifelines of virtual education. The availability of these resources directly impacts teachers' ability to deliver engaging and effective instruction to a diverse array of students, regardless of their geographic location or socioeconomic background.

Now, let's talk about equity in virtual education, but with a twist: each state is the author of its own policies in this virtual education saga. You see, when it comes to virtual education, it's not a one-size-fits-all scenario. Each state gets to make its own rules and decisions, and that includes how they fund it, regulate it, or even ban it.

Imagine it like this: it's a bit like a patchwork quilt, where some states are all in on virtual education, providing ample resources and support, while others might have restrictions or even prohibitions.

These state-level policies directly impact students' access to virtual learning and the quality of education they receive.

So when we discuss equity in virtual education, we're not just talking about equal access within a single system; we're navigating a complex landscape where the rules change from one state to another. Understanding these state-by-state variations is essential in ensuring that all students, regardless of where they live, have the same opportunities in the world of virtual education.

The Impact of Educational Policies

Educational policies and local regulations wield immense power in the realm of virtual education. They can promote innovation and flexibility or stifle progress. The decisions policymakers make about funding allocation, technology integration, and teacher professional development ripple through the virtual education landscape.

Empowering Educators

For educators navigating the dynamic world of virtual education, understanding the influence of educational policies and local regulations is not a luxury but a necessity. It equips them with the knowledge needed to advocate for the best interests of their students and themselves.

In the dynamic realm of virtual education, empowering educators is not merely a buzzword but a fundamental necessity. When we speak of empowering educators in this context, we're talking about providing them with the tools, knowledge, and support they need to navigate the complex interplay between governance and virtual education effectively.

Imagine educators as the captains of their virtual classrooms, steering their ships through uncharted waters. Governance acts as the navigational chart and compass, setting the course and outlining the boundaries. To empower these educators, we must ensure they not only understand these governing factors but also have a voice in shaping them.

> *In the face of a mass exodus of dedicated educators, we must confront the harsh reality that a lack of respect for the teaching profession is eroding the foundation of our education system. Teachers deserve more than just appreciation; they deserve to be recognized for their invaluable contributions. It's time to rebuild the respect and admiration for educators, in hopes that our schools can recover from this recent degradation of what American education has become.*
>
> Dr Eric Crespo, Superintendent,
> Weehawken Township School District

One way to empower educators is by involving them in the policymaking process. Their front-line experience equips them with invaluable insights into what works and what doesn't in the virtual classroom. When teachers actively participate in discussions and decisions regarding virtual education policies, it results in more realistic, student-centric, and effective governance.

Additionally, professional development plays a pivotal role in empowerment. Training programs that focus on virtual teaching techniques, technology integration, and understanding governance structures are essential. Empowered educators are not only more confident but also better equipped to advocate for their students and adapt to the ever-evolving virtual-education landscape.

Furthermore, providing educators with a clear understanding of the implications of governance decisions on their classrooms fosters a sense of agency. When educators can decipher how governance affects resource allocation, curriculum design, and access to technology, they become more informed advocates for equitable education.

Rebuilding our broken education system may seem a lofty goal. Teacher shortages, student struggles, achievement declines—where do we even begin? While there are no quick fixes, progress starts with communities united behind teachers and students. We all gain from strong public schools staffed by supported professionals. Collaboration around tangible solutions is key.

First, we need to truly listen to those on education's frontlines. Teachers, principals, counselors, support staff—their voices should lead the dialogue. They understand everyday realities and student needs. Top-down mandates by legislators or administrators fail because they lack classroom insights. Bring educators to the decision-making table.

Second, invest in our existing teachers. Celebrate their dedication and achievements. Make salaries competitive and restore respect. Provide mentorships, stipends for supplies, and opportunities for growth. Give teachers time to collaborate and freedom over curriculum. Reenergize the workforce by showing teachers their worth.

Fund improvements conveying education's value: modernized buildings, technology, training, diverse classes, support staff, interventions, enrichment programs. Lower class sizes and student-counselor ratios. Cease reliance on myopic metrics like standardized tests. Measure knowledge, not just skills. Let experienced teachers assess progress. Demonstrate commitment to fully preparing our next generation.

Finally, embrace innovation. Thoughtfully implement education technology to engage students and provide teacher flexibility. Connect virtual teachers to fill gaps. Offer hybrid models combining online and in-person learning. Personalize instruction and open access to electives. Blend digital tools with live teachers and supportive communities.

Change takes time, but progress begins with one step. Schools flourish when teachers do. Students thrive when given support that meets their individual needs. By standing united behind education, we secure the future. Our nation prospers through knowledge, empathy, and unity—qualities teachers instill. We owe it to children to ensure every classroom has a caring, committed professional guiding their potential. The solutions exist if we listen and dedicate the will to act.

Chapter Eleven

Ethics

Our lives begin to end the day we become silent about what matters.

Martin Luther King, Jr.

In the realm of education, ethical considerations take center stage, and the role of high-quality teachers becomes even more critical. As technology continues to revolutionize the educational landscape, educators must grapple with ethical challenges that emerge from the digital realm. Issues like student privacy, data security, equitable access to technology, and digital citizenship demand thoughtful consideration and responsible decision-making.

High-quality teachers, with their strong ethical compass, empathy, and commitment to student welfare, become the guardians of moral integrity within the classroom. Their dedication to upholding ethical standards not only ensures a safe and respectful learning environment but also nurtures students' character, empowering them to become responsible and principled digital citizens. In this context, valuing and empowering high-quality teachers becomes paramount as they serve as role models and advocates for ethical behavior, both online and offline, guiding students towards a future where technology is harnessed responsibly for the greater good.

If we want teachers to be stewards of knowledge and ensure ethical standards, then we have to make sure we are doing everything we can to create the best possible work environments for them to teach in.

For example, a college student might say: "I want to be a teacher."

If a school advisor responded truthfully, he or she might say something like: "Excellent choice. How do you feel about working a second job, 50+ hours per week at your teaching job, and do you cope well with workplace stress and abuse?"

Teachers who have been able to successfully transition out of the classroom said it felt like they were leaving a toxic and abusive relationship. It wasn't until they distanced themselves from the negligent work environment, over-demands, and underpayments that they understood what their minds and bodies had been through.

This is why it's important to build teachers up and recognize their roles as part of serving more than just education but society as a whole. #TeachersServeToo is about making a commitment to not simply recognize their service but to work towards building systemic change within the industry and within society. Our teachers deserve safe, ethical, and rewarding spaces to work within, not only because they work with our children but also because they are human beings. Teachers have sacrificed long enough, and it's our responsibility to show them that we not only recognize this sacrifice but that we have their backs in an industry that has become toxic and debilitating.

We need to start providing these would-be teachers with better scenarios. Pay alone is not the simple answer. Company culture and work-life balance are at the forefront of everyone's minds and hearts after the last few years. As we see employees returning back to the office or opting for work from home or hybrid options, education leaders have to truly consider that money is not the bottom line for most of their workers. The teacher transition movement speaks volumes about the education crisis, and we desperately need to listen to teachers. When both new and veteran educators are exiting their career paths in droves, it's not on them. How do we communicate that we know their value and worth and inspire others to follow in the footsteps of teaching?

A 2020 survey concluded 67 percent of teachers have a second and even third job. The average teacher works 50+ hours per week. Is there really any wonder we can't convince college students to pursue a teaching career?

By the time I left teaching, forty years had gone by and I had terrible urinary tract issues and had to see a specialist for my kidneys. Then, only two short years into retirement, I had to go back and start substitute teaching to cover my medical bills. The system does not care about us or our service.

Anonymous teacher

Setting Standards for Excellence from All: Leaders, Teachers, and (Gasp) Yes, Students and Their Families

Somewhere along the way we became a society of enablers of unethical behavior, completely numbed out to the situations, tragedies, and traumas taking place on our screens.

According to market research, The pandemic increased content usage by 207 percent as our social lives, kids' schools, and employment all moved online.

During that time, we became constant consumers of both light-hearted and visceral content as we watched the world cope with the ramifications of societal issues exacerbated by the lockdowns.

Maybe it was always there beneath the surface and wasn't blasted across television, computer, and phone screens; or maybe the constant stream of negative images got into our subconsciousness and began to take root.

Society can inadvertently become a breeding ground for enabling unethical conduct through various mechanisms. One significant factor is the normalization of behavior that might be ethically questionable or outright wrong. This normalization can occur when individuals witness others engaging in unethical actions without facing significant consequences, which leads them to believe that such behavior is acceptable.

Additionally, societal structures and institutions that prioritize short-term gains, competition, or individual success over collective well-being can contribute to enabling unethical conduct. When success is measured solely by metrics such as profit, power, or fame, individuals might feel pressured to cut corners, bend rules, or compromise their ethical principles to achieve these goals.

Lack of accountability mechanisms can also play a role. If there's a lack of transparency, oversight, or consequences for unethical behavior, individuals might feel emboldened to engage in such conduct, knowing that they are unlikely to face repercussions.

Social biases and cognitive dissonance can further enable unethical conduct. People tend to rationalize their actions and find justifications for behavior that aligns with their self-interest, even if it goes against their stated ethical values.

Media and social media can amplify these dynamics. Misleading information, sensationalism, or the glorification of unethical behavior can desensitize people to the moral implications of such actions.

Whatever is the cause of our constant degradation of each other and society, it's time to flip the switch.

What Do We Owe to Each Other?

In T. M. Scanlon's book, *What We Owe to Each Other*, philosopher and professor emeritus at Harvard University delves into questions of how we justify our moral judgements and actions.

He inevitably concludes that "What we owe each other" encapsulates the fundamental principles of reciprocity, empathy, and ethical responsibility that underpin harmonious human interactions. It signifies a moral obligation to treat one another with respect, fairness, and consideration, recognizing the shared humanity that binds us together. We need this sentiment now more than ever, especially in our schools and classrooms.

This concept encompasses both the tangible debts of kindness and support we owe to those around us, as well as the intangible debts of understanding and compassion that contribute to the social fabric. It suggests that in the complex web of relationships and interconnectedness, we are duty-bound to foster a sense of community, contribute positively to the lives of others, and work collectively towards a better world. By acknowledging what we owe each other, we acknowledge our interconnectedness and strive to build a society grounded in empathy and mutual support.

Education leaders can play a crucial role in fostering ethical behavior within the education system by demonstrating strong ethical leadership and implementing policies that prioritize the well-being and development of students, educators, and the broader community. Here are some ways education leaders can be more ethical:

Lead by Example. Education leaders should model ethical behavior in their actions and decisions. Their integrity, honesty, and transparency set the tone for the entire educational community.

Prioritize Student Well-being. Put students' physical, mental, and emotional well-being at the forefront of decision-making.

Create a safe and inclusive environment that promotes positive student development.

Equitable Practices. Strive for equity and inclusion in all aspects of education. Ensure that resources, opportunities, and support are distributed fairly among all students, regardless of their background.

Promote Academic Integrity. Uphold academic honesty and integrity by educating students about plagiarism, proper citation, and the importance of original work.

Support Educators. Provide adequate training, professional development, and support for educators. Recognize their contributions and address issues like low pay, heavy workloads, and lack of resources.

Cultivate Ethical Decision-Making. Encourage critical thinking and ethical decision-making skills among students and educators. Offer opportunities for discussions on ethical dilemmas and complex issues.

Transparent Communication. Maintain open lines of communication with students, educators, parents, and the community. Transparency helps build trust and ensures that stakeholders are informed about important decisions.

Diverse and Inclusive Curriculum. Develop a curriculum that reflects diverse cultures, perspectives, and experiences. Teach students about empathy, tolerance, and respect for different viewpoints.

Data Privacy. Safeguard students' and educators' personal data. Implement strong data privacy policies to protect sensitive information.

Address Bullying and Harassment. Have robust antibullying and antiharassment policies in place. Create a culture where bullying is not tolerated and there are clear avenues for reporting and addressing such incidents.

Ethical Use of Technology. Promote responsible and ethical use of technology in education, including respecting students' digital privacy and addressing issues like cyberbullying.

Collaboration and Consultation. Involve stakeholders in decision-making processes. Seek input from educators, students, parents, and community members to ensure that diverse perspectives are considered.

Be an Advocate for Change. Address systemic issues in education, such as funding disparities, by advocating for policy changes that prioritize equitable resources and opportunities.

Continuous Improvement and Growth Mindset. Regularly assess the effectiveness of policies and practices and be willing to make necessary adjustments to align with ethical principles.

Promote Ethical Development. Implement programs that nurture students' ethical development, emphasizing values like honesty, empathy, and responsibility.

By embracing these principles and taking proactive steps, education leaders can create an ethical culture within their institutions that supports the holistic growth and success of all stakeholders involved in the education system.

Will Artificial Intelligence Replace Teachers?

The short is answer: No.

While AI technology continues to advance and play an increasingly prominent role in education, AI cannot completely replace classroom teachers. The essence of effective teaching extends beyond the mere dissemination of information. Classroom educators provide invaluable guidance, mentorship, and personalized support that foster holistic development in students. Teachers offer emotional intelligence, adaptability, and the ability to tailor their approach to accommodate diverse learning styles and individual needs, creating a dynamic and interactive learning environment that AI, despite its capabilities, cannot fully replicate.

The human touch in education, characterized by empathy, motivation, and the cultivation of critical thinking and social skills, remains an indispensable component that ensures the holistic growth of students and prepares them to navigate the complexities of the real world.

A collaborative approach should be taken to discover what AI can do for teachers and students, but all within the realm of ethical approaches and an exploratory nature. This might take some time as teachers and students learn how best to use this technology. The education sector stands to benefit immensely from a collaborative partnership with AI technology, enhancing and optimizing educational practices.

By leveraging AI's data analysis capabilities, educators can gain valuable insights into students' learning patterns, identifying areas of strength and weakness. This enables them to tailor instructional strategies to individual needs, promoting personalized and adaptive learning experiences. AI-powered tools can also automate administrative tasks, freeing up educators' time to focus on more impactful aspects of teaching, such as interactive discussions and fostering critical thinking. Furthermore, AI-driven virtual tutors and educational platforms can provide supplementary resources, enabling students to learn at their own pace while receiving immediate feedback. Embracing AI in education encourages innovation, helps bridge learning gaps, and equips students with essential digital skills, ultimately creating a symbiotic relationship where technology complements and amplifies the expertise of educators for the betterment of educational outcomes.

I think of these advances in AI as an opportunity for successful renewal in education. Human teachers will always be necessary to provide specific content feedback and support. But in areas of need, AI may be a productive and pragmatic way to manage a school schedule and help provide students with the basics. That can lead to true renewal and improvement.

AI also plays an important role in helping teachers maximize instructional resources to meet the needs of students nationally. With advanced technology, we may be able to use individual avatars and AI to teach content and interact with students dynamically. Much of that technology is on the brink of being successful.

Consider online chatbots, for example, and their ability to interact with potential or existing customers. It portends a range of future possibilities.

With this in mind, research the best AI resources that may be a fit for your school. They should reflect democratic student choice, balanced with privacy and security. You may also consider looking at online courses as another means of invigorating your educational program. Massive open online courses (MOOCs) are becoming more prevalent in colleges, and they could be an example for how K–12 programming will evolve in the future.

The need for rapid change and retooling student skill sets in a tech-enabled world makes MOOCs stand out as providers of the kind of flexibility in programming that characterizes educational renewal today. Helping students update their skills and providing them with the insight they need to critically enhance their ability to be competitive in their future careers is essential in today's fast-paced, global economic terrain.

While AI can enhance various aspects of learning, teachers provide an essential human connection that nurtures not only academic growth but also character development, emotional intelligence, and the cultivation of critical life skills. The role of a teacher encompasses mentorship, inspiration, and fostering a sense of community within the classroom by creating an environment where students feel valued, motivated, and empowered to reach their full potential. As we embrace the benefits of AI in education, we must remember that the heart of education lies in the hands of dedicated educators who serve as guiding lights, shaping the future of our society through their unwavering commitment to nurturing well-rounded individuals.

Conclusion

O ur country faces no shortage of divisive issues. Education rarely makes headlines and when it does, it's never "good news."

Yet, ensuring every student reaches their potential impacts all aspects of society. Teacher shortages threaten the very backbone of our future, which is an informed, compassionate, engaged citizenry. We dismiss education at our collective peril.

Proximity Learning Inc. originated to tackle these shortages using technology to engage teachers and learners. But startups alone cannot overhaul entrenched systems. Real change requires all stakeholders—parents, communities, administrators, legislators, even local businesses—to elevate access to public education as a priority. Only by working in partnership and listening to those directly shaping young lives can we transform schools into supportive environments where teachers and students thrive.

There are no quick fixes. However, progress begins by agreeing: our children deserve access to caring, qualified teachers. This is the least we can provide for a generation of students that will inevitably inherit a world in need of saving and healing. They deserve schools inspiring them to discover passions, leverage strengths, and respect differences. They deserve the chance to fulfill their promise without limitations imposed by staff shortages and system inertia. Education can equip the next generation to conquer humanity's greatest challenges. But first, we must ensure every classroom has a compassionate professional guiding the way. We need teachers in place who aren't afraid to challenge the status quo, and most importantly, we need to support these teachers as they take on one of the most important jobs in the world: teaching.

I don't claim to have all the answers. But this much I know: America has phenomenal teachers with the ability to change lives. My mother was one. The problem is not teachers but the structures failing them. With creativity and commitment, we can rebuild an education system teachers are proud to be part of and students are excited to attend.

The teacher shortage is a call to action, one I sincerely hope you will join. We cannot waiver until quality education is a reality for all. The future beckons; our students are ready. With united passion, optimism, and hard work, we will get there. The journey begins today.

#TeachersServeToo

#TeachersServeToo is more than a hashtag, it's a resonant call to action that transcends fleeting trends. It represents a collective recognition of the pivotal role teachers play in shaping the foundation of our society. Beyond a timely movement, it encapsulates a profound understanding of the intricate dynamics within education. This rallying cry signifies a commitment to usher in the transformative shift that public education urgently requires. It's a declaration that goes beyond lip service, demonstrating our dedication to investing in the very essence of learning—the educators themselves. By championing this cause, we affirm that teachers' value extends far beyond the classroom walls; they are architects of intellect, mentors of character, and builders of the future. As we stand behind the notion that "teachers serve too," we invigorate a renaissance of education, spotlighting the tireless efforts, unyielding dedication, and boundless impact teachers have on generations to come.

Appendix

Learner Engagement Playbook

Purpose

To help you consistently engage learners in behaviors that optimize their learning experiences and increase their time on task with active strategies.

Our wish for you is to leverage this guide and find opportunities to apply the strategies within the discipline and courses you teach. As a result, we will maximize the flow of student learning from the minute class starts (your bell ringer) to the minute class ends (your exit ticket).

Bell-Ringer	Presenting Your Instructional Content	Exit Tickets

Remember, if students are not engaged, they are not learning. To ensure that students are actively engaging with content (rather than passively receiving it), it is valuable to design instruction with the five facets of student motivation in mind. How can you improve your instructional delivery while encompassing more of these five facets?

1. **Autonomy.** Classrooms that are set up to operate self-sufficiently and include more learner choice will stimulate engagement.
2. **Competence.** The more learners believe they can be successful, the more they will engage in your class.

3. **Emotions.** Interest in a learning activity is developed when interactions produce positive feedback. Learners interested in the experiences you facilitate, and that they have some autonomy over, will show greater attention, have a recall of facts, and persistence.
4. **Relationships.** Positive interactions with you, and between student to student, will energize your learners and engage them.
5. **Value.** Learners will be more motivated to learn when they feel the experiences we are providing them have relevance, meaning, and connect to their lives.

Sample Bell-ringer Engagement Strategies			
What	**How**	**Why**	**Student Motivation**
Get a Clue	Find clues (images, problems, key words) about the new lesson and paste them on a slide for students to view. Have the students discuss or write what they think the topic of the day is based on the clues provided.	Embraces prior knowledge and encourages curiosity	Competence
Musical Notes	Instruct your students to find their notes from the previous class day. The teacher plays music while the students walk around the room. When the music stops, students pair up with the classmate closest to them, trade notes, and summarize the notes out loud to their partner.	Encourages students to look at their notes from the day before and supports summarization skills.	Emotions

Discussion Boards	Whether via a live dialogue or a static post in the discussion forum, generate a thought-provoking prompt to spark curiosity.	Stimulates critical thinking skills	Relationships

Bell-Ringers (Start of Class)

Many refer to the first five minutes of a class as the most important. Why? The first five minutes set the tone and purpose for the rest of the learning to occur.

Also known as warm-ups, bell work, participatory hooks, do-nows, openers, entry-tickets, or jump starters, a bell ringer is the short activity that students do upon entering the classroom. They may be standards-driven, spiral review-orientated, inspirational, challenging, or even game-like. Bell-ringers are more than just "something students do while you check roll"; they are the engine to the classroom train, the secret sauce to setting the tone, and the trick to calming the chaos.

What are some benefits of bell-ringers?

- Engaging students in short assignments or assessments
- Reviewing key concepts already taught
- Stimulating class discussion that supports your lesson
- Identifying misconceptions and misunderstandings your learners may have

What are some tips that lead to bell-ringer success?

- Develop structure and consistency with your bell-ringers. Familiarity with your process and learner expectations will help you maximize the first five minutes of class and get your learners into a routine.

- Hold your learners accountable. Create a culture of understanding where your class understands that these activities are not busy work but an important part of their learning process.

- Assign meaningful activities. Plan backward with your learning goals in mind and develop your bellringer to fuel the rest of your planned lesson.

Presenting Instructional Content (Middle of Class)

Instructional engagement strategies are like the glue that binds a virtual classroom together. They are essential tools for educators to captivate students' attention, foster active participation, and enhance learning outcomes. Just as a skilled conductor leads an orchestra to harmonious music, these strategies orchestrate a cohesive and effective learning experience in the digital realm. They create a dynamic and interactive environment where students feel connected, motivated, and eager to learn, making virtual education more engaging and successful.

What are some benefits of engagement strategies?

- **Improved Learning.** Engagement strategies enhance student comprehension and retention.

- **Active Participation.** They encourage students to interact with the material and with peers.

- **Motivation.** These strategies inspire students to stay engaged and complete their tasks.

- **Varied Learning Styles.** They cater to diverse learning preferences and foster. inclusivity.

- **Real-world Application.** Engagement strategies help students apply knowledge to practical scenarios.

What are some tips that lead to successful implementation of engagement strategies?

- **Clear Objectives.** Define clear learning objectives for each engagement strategy to ensure alignment with your educational goals.

- **Student-Centered Approach.** Tailor engagement strategies to suit the needs, interests, and learning styles of your students.

- **Effective Technology.** Choose and use appropriate technology and tools that support your chosen engagement strategies and the virtual-learning environment.

- **Feedback Loop.** Regularly assess the effectiveness of your strategies and adapt them based on student feedback and performance data.

- **Professional Development.** Invest in ongoing professional development to stay current with the latest engagement strategies and best practices in online teaching.

Appendix

Presenting Instructional Content Engagement Strategies			
What	**How**	**Why**	**Student Motivation**
Exemplars and Non-exemplars Showcasing different levels of work	Curate a collection of anonymous work examples. Allow students to view the examples in groups and discuss which one earns the highest/lowest grade and the reasons why.	Increases awareness of different levels of performance and allows for student self-reflection	Competence
Guided Notes	Share guided notes template. During the lesson, prompt students to interact with the notes, filling in information and discussing key concepts. Afterward, review the notes together to reinforce understanding and use them as a for-mative assessment tool.	Guided notes enhance focus, comprehension, and engagement for virtual learners.	Competence
Growth Mindset Culture	Create a classroom climate that recognizes that mistakes are essential to learning. Prompt ChatGPT for ways to incorporate Growth Mindset into lessons.	Reinforces effort, not ability	Competence
Movement	Incorporate light physical activities within your daily lessons.	Increases participation and keeps students interested	Emotion

Exit Tickets (End of Class)

One of the last steps to wrapping a present is tying the bow. Think of exit slips as tying the bow on the day's learning. As your bell-ringer starts the class, your exit slip is a natural way to end the class. Exit slips are one of the easiest ways to obtain information about students' current levels of understanding.

What are some benefits of exit tickets? They:

- Allow you to quickly check for learner comprehension.

- Provide you a snapshot to guide your next day's instruction. Did many learners struggle with the exit ticket? If yes, you can use the next class period to review key concepts before moving forward in your thematic units.

- Assist you in organizing your learners into groups: students who fully understood the lesson, students who partially understood, and those who did not understand the concept at all.

- Promote learner accountability because students know that at the end of a lesson they will have an opportunity to prove their level of mastery.

- Promote learner engagement.

- Help clarify the main concept of the lesson. Students quickly realize that whatever concept was included in the exit ticket was the MAIN concept of the lesson.

- Allow learners to ask questions in a nonthreatening way. Some students may be uncomfortable asking a question during class, but the exit ticket provides them a safe space to share with you what they need support with.

Exit Ticket Engagement Strategies			
What	**How**	**Why**	**Student Motivation**
Tic Tac Toe—Student Choice Exit Ticket	Make a tic-tac-toe board with a range of leveled questions or problems to solve. Columns 1–3 increase in challenge level. Students choose three squares to solve for tic tac toe! Try Nearpod Draw It for Tic Tac Toe.	Motivates by allowing student choice in a game format. Meets all level learners by providing differentiated questions.	Autonomy
What stuck with you today?	Ask students that one simple question to prompt them to write something that made the greatest impact from the day's lesson. When applicable, extend their thinking to include, "Why?"	Promotes self-reflection and provides formative feedback.	Autonomy
3-2-1	Students share three things they learned, two things they found interesting, and one question they have.	Forces students to self-reflect and take autonomy over their learning	Autonomy/ Competence

Yesterday's News	Students summarize today's lesson using detailed examples, as if writing a news article for tomorrow's "headline" warm-up. The teacher gathers, assesses, and shares several chosen [anonymous] samples at the beginning of next day's lesson.	Serves as both an assessment of learning objectives and a means to activate prior knowledge at the start of class. Fosters enthusiasm for participation in the warm-up.	Competence
Emoji Exit Ticket	Ask students to pick an emoji and explain why it represents how they are feeling about their understanding of the lesson. Responses can be in the chat, on a Nearpod Collaborate board, Padlet, or teacher-created form.	Promotes metacognition. Students connect with the lesson and share their progress.	Emotions

About the Contributors

Dr. Shawn Joseph

Dr. Shawn Joseph's passion for equity and social justice has led him to serve in a number of positions in the world of education. He has been an English teacher, reading specialist, school administrator, central office administrator, and superintendent in Delaware (Seaford School District) and Tennessee (Metro Nashville Public Schools). He served on the faculty of Fordham University in the Department of Educational Leadership, Administration, and Policy during the 2019 to 2020 school year and is currently Co-Director of the AASA/Howard Urban Superintendent Academy and Assistant Professor of Educational Leadership, Administration, and Policy Studies at Howard University.

In 2019 and 2020, Dr. Joseph was selected as the Person of the Year by the Tribune Newspaper in Nashville. His first book, *The Principal's Guide to the First 100 Days of the School Year: Creating Instructional Momentum*, offers insight into the complexity of the principalship and suggests strategies for focusing on increasing student achievement. In 2019, he published the book *Finding the Joseph Within*, a memoir which tells the account of his professional journey and how faith and perseverance unleashed favor upon his life.

Dr. Jermall Wright

As an experienced turnaround school principal, Dr. Wright led two elementary schools out of turnaround status through strategic partnerships, community and parental engagement, data-driven instruction, student and adult culture, and a focus on early literacy. In 2013, he joined the Denver Public Schools as an instructional superintendent responsible for leading the turnaround efforts of chronically underperforming elementary schools. By 2016, 75 percent of Denver's turnaround schools under Dr. Wright's leadership improved by at least two performance tiers, moving them off the district's intervention list.

In 2017, Dr. Wright joined the Birmingham, Alabama, City School District as the chief academic and accountability officer, where he led the school improvement process. Under his leadership, the system decreased the number of "F-rated" schools from twenty-two to six and increased the number of schools rated "C" or above from six to seventeen. On April 11, 2019, the Mississippi State Board of Education appointed Dr. Wright as the founding superintendent of the Mississippi Achievement School District, serving Yazoo City and Humphreys County. In three years, graduation rates improved from 67 percent to 85 percent in Yazoo City and from 78 percent to 91 percent in Humphreys County.

In addition to his work as an accomplished school and central-level educational leader, Dr. Wright is also an experienced college/university instructor, having served in teacher preparation programs at Florida State College at Jacksonville, Florida, and Trinity University, Washington, DC; affiliate faculty of special education and educational leadership at Regis University, Denver, CO; and contributing faculty in Walden University's EdD/PhD program in early childhood.

Dr. Anna Stubblefield

Dr. Anna Stubblefield became the twenty-second superintendent of schools for Kansas City, Kansas, Public Schools on July 1, 2021. As a proven and focused leader, she understands the importance of building effective leadership teams, increasing community outreach, and fostering vital partnerships within the community that encourages and support academic achievement.

Dr. Stubblefield earned her doctorate in educational leadership from Saint Louis University, an educational specialist's degree from the University of Missouri at Kansas City, and two masters degrees (special education and teaching & leadership) along with her bachelor's degree in education from the University of Kansas.

Dr. J. R. Green

A native South Carolinian, Dr. J. R. Green has served the students of South Carolina in the capacity of teacher, assistant principal, principal, assistant superintendent, and superintendent for twenty-five years. Green has served the Fairfield County School District for eleven years. During his tenure, he guided the construction of a new career center and launched a dual enrollment for high school students that would allow them to graduate high school with an associates degree from Midlands Tech.

Dr. Green launched the STEM Early College Academy initiative. This was a partnership with Midlands Technical College that provided Fairfield County students the opportunity to graduate high school with an associates degree in science. One of the proudest moments of Dr. Green's tenure is the recognition of Fairfield Central High teacher, Ms. Chanda Jefferson, as the 2020 South Carolina State Teacher of the Year. Ms. Jefferson's recognition is the first time the district has had a state teacher of the year.

Dr. Victoria Hansen Stockton

Dr. Hansen Stockton is a transformational educational leader with over thirteen years of experience in Bellwood School District 88. She coined her core philosophical beliefs in education as the 3-E Platform. This platform has become the basis on which the organization operates and will drive continued success in the district.

Dr. Hansen Stockton is committed to forging a new competitive path for students and staff that will resound within the greater educational community of Proviso Township and beyond.

Dr. Ingrid Grant

Dr. Ingrid Grant is a distinguished and visionary educator, currently serving as the Chief of School Leadership for Henrico County Public Schools, where her transformative leadership has left an indelible mark on the educational landscape. With a career dedicated to pursuing excellence in education, Dr. Grant has amassed a wealth of experience and expertise. Her journey began with a fervent commitment to fostering an inclusive and innovative learning environment. Driven by a passion for empowering educators and students, she has consistently championed initiatives prioritizing equity, diversity, and student success.

Her extensive background includes pivotal roles such as a principal, successfully turning around two Title I schools, an assistant principal for an alternative elementary/middle school, and an exceptional education teacher at both the elementary and secondary levels. She has been the Director of School Improvement and Middle School Education in her distinguished career, collaborating with principals to enhance teaching and learning outcomes.

Dr. Grant's remarkable contributions have been recognized through accolades such as the 2009 R.E.B. Award for Distinguished Educational Leadership while serving as principal of Ratcliffe Elementary, the 2018 Instructional Leader of the Year for Henrico County Public School and being named a Time Dispatch 2020 Honoree for Person of the Year. Under her leadership, the schools she led received several awards at the local and state levels for outstanding academic performance as Title I institutions.

In addition to her impactful roles in education, Dr. Grant has been actively involved in various committees at the county and state levels and has been a presenter at conferences on local, state, national, and university platforms. Notably, in 2019, she was appointed to the

Virginia Governor's first African American Advisory Board, further showcasing her commitment to shaping educational policies and practices.

Devin Del Palacio

Devin Del Palacio is a member of the governing board of the Tolleson Union High School District, covering the cities of Tolleson, Avondale, and Phoenix, Arizona. Devin was raised by a single mother, and due to financial situations, attended eight different public schools while growing up. He was taught the value of hard work from a young age and was raised to take positive action in his community. Seeking the opportunity to give back, Devin became a community organizer in 2012, working for the next few years to empower and register 34,000 minority voters in South and West Phoenix.

In 2014, Devin decided to run for a seat on the Tolleson Union High School District Governing Board. He won and immediately became the vice president of the board. In his first 120 days in office, Devin worked to bring the My Brother's Keeper Initiative to the Tolleson district, with the goal of creating positive educational and life outcomes for young men of color. Since then, Devin has worked to ensure that the Tolleson district becomes a safe and successful place for all students, by introducing policies and resolutions to support diverse students and to create new opportunities for students. In 2017, he championed the passage of the Tolleson Union High School Bond campaign, which was overwhelmingly approved by district voters. Currently, TUHSD is a growing district, constructing a new high school campus and expanding opportunities for west valley students.

Devin serves as chairman of the Black Council for National School Board Association. He works to increase academic achievement for ethnic and racial minority groups and to support diverse school board members in their communities. Closer to home, he serves as the chair of the Black Caucus of the Arizona School Boards Association and vice president of the NAACP Arizona Chapter. Devin recently joined the board of Young Voices for the Planet.

Micah Ali

Born and reared in Compton, California, Micah Ali brings a keen grasp of the complex issues facing urban schools to help champion working families, students and urban communities by responding effectively to educational inequities based upon racial, ethnic and socio-economic differences. Currently serving his 12th year on the Compton Unified School District Board of Trustees, Mr. Ali operates at the nexus of business and government, where he specializes in developing and promoting successful and mutually beneficial public-private partnerships. Dedicated to eliminating the achievement gap, permanently dismantling the school-to-prison pipeline and addressing these challenges on multiple formats, Ali also serves on the California Racial and Identity Profiling Advisory (RIPA) Commission. He is also the inaugural-president of the California Association of Black School Educators – an organization spanning traditional schools, charters and community colleges for the singular purpose of educational equity for Black students; and is Chair-Emeritus of the Council of Urban Boards of Education.

In the past, Ali also served on the Board of Directors for the California School Boards Association (CSBA) and National School Boards Association (NSBA). Recognizing the structures that perpetuate inequality in education, through this latter position, he was responsible for creating and pushing NSBA's vision for educational equity, addressing assumptions about how students of color learn and creating opportunities for more children to succeed nationwide. Ali received his Bachelor of Science from California State University, Dominguez Hills and earned his Master of Arts in Education School Administration from Loyola Marymount University.

Dr. Eric Crespo

Dr. Eric Crespo, a Bronx native and North Bergen resident, was raised by parents who immigrated from Cuba. Since 2018, he has served as the Superintendent of Schools for Weehawken Public

Schools in New Jersey. Prior to his role in Weehawken, he worked as an assistant superintendent for Paterson Public Schools, the second-largest school district in New Jersey.

During his tenure in Weehawken Schools, the district has garnered numerous awards and accolades from various organizations, including:

- Lighthouse Award for Special Education Post-Secondary Success
- Digital Star Schools recognition
- Sustainable Schools designation
- AP CSP Female Diversity recognition
- Namm Award for Best in Music Education
- Tech and Learning Innovative Leader Award
- NJASA executive member
- Garden State Coalition trustee district member
- NJAEL Trustee District member
- Model School 2023
- Niche rated Weehawken Schools as the #1 district in Hudson County and the #25 High School in the state

Dr. Crespo has been instrumental in leading the statewide AI Committee and is overseeing the addition of the district's first electric bus to its fleet during the upcoming winter. Furthermore, he successfully led two referendums, each receiving over 80% approval, and is currently overseeing the construction of a new school.

In addition to his administrative responsibilities, Dr. Crespo is an accomplished keynote speaker and educational presenter, covering a range of topics. He has initiated programs such as aviation, special education, a fully functional bank, aquaponics, hydroponics, and an apiary within the district.

Notably, Dr. Crespo is in the final stages of completing his doctoral dissertation at St. Peter's University, focusing on the effectiveness of professional development in schools, with an expected completion date in the Fall of 2024.

One of the highlights of Dr. Crespo's daily routine is visiting classrooms, engaging with teachers, and providing support to families in his community.

About the Author

Evan is a visionary entrepreneur and education advocate who stands at the forefront of a transformative movement in online learning. As the founder of Proximity Learning, he has dedicated his career to bridging the gap between technology and education, reimagining the possibilities of virtual classrooms, and empowering educators and students across the globe.

With a profound belief in the power of innovation to reshape traditional paradigms, Evan embarked on a mission to revolutionize the educational landscape. Armed with a deep understanding of the challenges facing education systems, he set out to create a solution that would leverage the potential of digital platforms, while preserving the essence of quality instruction.

Under Evan's leadership, Proximity Learning has flourished into a beacon of change, offering a dynamic platform that connects passionate educators with students regardless of geographical boundaries. This groundbreaking approach addresses the pressing need for qualified teachers in underserved communities and opens doors for students to access a world-class education, regardless of their location.

About Proximity Learning

Proximity Learning offers a comprehensive suite of services that replicate the experience of in-person instruction, encompassing standard classes, tutoring, and summer school across a wide spectrum of subjects. Their extensive catalog of courses covers core subjects, specialty courses, special education (SPED), and speech-language pathology areas. Guided by the values of passion, innovation, and integrity, Proximity Learning continuously explores novel approaches to impact students positively.

The genesis of Proximity Learning dates back to the late 00s when video calls gained popularity. Recognizing the potential of video technology as an instructional tool, Proximity Learning envisioned a transformative shift in education. The benefits of live instruction, including eye contact, facial expressions, and dynamic interactions, were undeniable, and this realization laid the foundation for their journey.

In the 2010s, as the teacher vacancy crisis unfolded, Proximity Learning discovered its mission. They understood that it was now feasible to connect certified teachers from one part of the country to students in another, breaking geographical barriers. This innovative approach gave schools access to certified teachers from across the nation, ensuring greater educational equity for students in diverse districts. Their core mission is to connect all learners with the expert teachers they deserve, ultimately enhancing educational equity to enable every child to reach their full potential.

The Proximity Learning team brings together diverse backgrounds from various facets of the education landscape, including teaching, public school administration, higher education, education technology companies, staffing organizations, and more. United by their passion for making a difference, they continually seek new avenues to increase educational equity.

Committed to principles of empowerment, transparency, and honesty, Proximity Learning prioritizes strong relationships with clients, content employees, and substantive progress in connecting students nationwide with certified teachers. Their belief in the power of empowerment extends to teachers, providing them with a robust support network to thrive and make a meaningful impact.

Proximity Learning's mission and core values were formulated collectively, with input from employees across all levels and teams within the organization. They take pride in being guided by the aspirations of their dedicated team, which is unwavering in its commitment to transforming the education landscape.

To provide students with the most interactive, dynamic, and effective education possible, Proximity Learning equips its teachers with cutting-edge digital tools. These educators prioritize engagement and effectiveness, leveraging interactive education platforms like Kahoot and Nearpod, and honing their communication skills.

Recognizing the challenges schools face in offering a wide range of courses, Proximity Learning offers the opportunity to partner with them to provide specialty classes on a period-by-period basis. This includes advanced placement (AP) courses in subjects such as biology, US history, and statistics, as well as career and technical education courses like culinary arts and entrepreneurship.

Comprehensive support is available at every step of the journey. Proximity Learning's support team assists school administrators, teachers, students, and parents to ensure a seamless and enriching learning experience. Their commitment to combining experience, quality, and technology results in classrooms that engage students and promote educational equity.

Proximity Learning is dedicated to reshaping education, one virtual classroom at a time. They invite individuals and institutions to join them in their mission to make high-quality education accessible to all, regardless of geographical boundaries or resource constraints.

Printed in the USA
CPSIA information can be obtained
at www.ICGtesting.com
JSHW061934280224
58160JS00005B/10